TAKING
OUR CITIES
FOR GOD

TAKING OUR CITIES FOR GOD

JOHN DAWSON

WORD PUBLISHING

Word (UK) Ltd
Milton Keynes, England

WORD AUSTRALIA
Kilsyth, Victoria, Australia

STRUIK CHRISTIAN BOOKS (PTY) LTD
Maitland, South Africa

ALBY COMMERCIAL ENTERPRISES PTE LTD
Balmoral Road, Singapore

CHRISTIAN MARKETING NEW ZEALAND LTD
Havelock North, New Zealand

JENSCO LTD
Hong Kong

SALVATION BOOK CENTRE
Malaysia

TAKING OUR CITIES FOR GOD

© 1989 by John Dawson

First published in the USA by Creation House Publishers, Florida.
First UK edition 1991 by Word (UK) Ltd.
All rights reserved.
No part of this publication may be reproduced or transmitted in any form or by any means, electronic or mechanical, including photocopy, recording, or any information storage or retrieval system, without permission in writing from the Publisher.

ISBN 0-85009-242-6 (Australia ISBN 1-86258-129-0)

Reproduced, printed and bound in Great Britain for Word (UK) Ltd. by Cox & Wyman Ltd., Reading, Berks.

94 / 10 9 8 7 6 5

To the urban missionaries
on Youth With a Mission teams
around the world.

Acknowledgments

I wish to thank Jim and Joy Dawson, my parents, who taught me to know God and make Him known; Loren Cunningham, who taught me to think in terms of the big picture; and Winkie Pratney, who taught me to study human culture with compassion.

I am deeply indebted to Andy and Marcia Zimmermann for running my office and typing this manuscript and to my dear wife, Julie. along with our children, David, Paul and Matthew. This book is their story too.

Contents

Foreword 11

SECTION ONE
BATTLE STORIES

1 Seventh Time Around 17
2 The Discerning of Spirits 23

SECTION TWO
DELIVER THE DARK CITY

3 A Call to the City 33
4 Cities: A Blessing or a Curse? 39
5 Ministering in the City of the Future 47
6 Revival or Judgment—What Will It Be? 57
7 The City at Harvest Time 69

SECTION THREE
DISCERNING THE GATES OF YOUR CITY

8 Looking at History With Discernment 77
9 The History of God's People/Covenants 87
10 Prophets, Intercessors and Spiritual Fathers 97
11 Get the Facts 111

SECTION FOUR
LEARNING TO FIGHT

12 Born to Battle.. 125
13 The Unseen Realm... 133
14 Praying in the Presence of the Heavenly
Host.. 137
15 All About Angels.. 143
16 Territorial Spirits.. 149

SECTION FIVE
INTO BATTLE: FIVE STEPS TO VICTORY

17 Worship: The Place of Beginnings............... 161
18 Waiting on the Lord for Insight.................... 169
19 Identifying With the Sins of the City........... 181
20 Overcoming Evil With Good.......................... 189
21 Travailing Until Birth..................................... 201

STUDY GUIDE   219

Foreword

It is an honour to write the foreword for this book. John Dawson is a personal friend and I have had the privilege of standing beside him in ministry on many occasions around the world.

I commend this book to you for several vital reasons. First of all, John lives out the message that he teaches. He lives in a city that he is taking for God! He has committed himself to the city of Los Angeles by living in one of its needier neighbourhoods, yet he has not treated his neighbours as objects of paternalistic compassion. Rather, he has treated them as friends.

This book is a timely message from God. Occasionally a book comes along that is more than a good book, it is indeed a word from God. This is such a book. God has already anointed this book around the world. Whole denominations have asked every pastor to read it. The evangelical alliance in some nations have distributed copies to every spiritual leader. This book, more than any other I have read in years, has the potential to affect the destiny of cities and nations for God.

The third reason why this book is so important, is

that it builds hope and faith for the city. Not only does it teach us God's ways in taking our cities for Him, but as we put those ways into practice it creates a sense of anticipation of what God is going to do through us. John shares stories of what God has taught him from real life experiences – experiences that ring true.

I remember going out with John to a favourite Mexican restaurant that he has taken me to on several occasions in Los Angeles. John handed me a copy of the manuscript when it was not yet completed. As I read through the pages of the book to be I was deeply moved. "This is the book that I have wanted to write," I said to myself. I must admit I was a little jealous, yet at the same time extremely grateful to have had the privilege of seeing the book in its earliest form. I commended John for his outstanding work, and encouraged him to go on. I knew he had a word from the Lord. He has certainly been inspired by the Holy Spirit and I know you too will be as you prayerfully study what God has to say to us through my friend, John Dawson.

Floyd McClung

TAKING OUR CITIES FOR GOD

SECTION ONE

BATTLE STORIES

Breaking through a city's invisible barriers
to the gospel

*"Michael, one of the chief princes, came to help
me, for I had been left alone there with the kings
of Persia. "*
Daniel 10:13

ONE

Seventh Time Around

"For the weapons of our warfare are not carnal but mighty in God for pulling down strongholds." 2 Corinthians 10:4

The torch flared in my hand as I picked up speed. Sweat glistened on the other runners as they passed beneath the street lamps of Century City. "I claim the resources of the west side for You, Lord! May the wealth, talent and influence of this city be used to proclaim Your love."

The tiny cluster of runners moved on into the night, grateful to know the Pacific Ocean was only twenty-eight blocks away but dreading the thought that such a great adventure was coming to an end. Starting their journey at Plymouth Rock they had run from the East Coast to the West Coast as an act of intercessory prayer, claiming America's new generation for Jesus.

Along the way they had been joined by thousands of children and teens who ran with flaming torches symbolising the light of the gospel.

I passed off the torch to my thirteen-year-old son, David. Does he really understand what we are doing? I thought. Is he beginning to comprehend the vast love of a heavenly Father who longs to pour healing, justice and mercy into the earth if we simply humble ourselves and ask for it?

A man exited a bar, stood on the pavement and stared at the runners in amazement. After all, it was after midnight. "We're running for Jesus," shouted a teenager and an amused smirk crossed the face of the bar patron. I could almost hear him thinking: those crazy Christians, what do they hope to achieve?

God's people sometimes do crazy things, things that only make sense when seen with the eyes of faith. We are called to be salt and light, transforming the world around us, but the source of our power is invisible. The infinite meets the finite in the simple obedience of a believer's life.

I thought back to my first experience of seeing a city change through the power of prayer. It was Cordoba, Argentina, 1978.

We were frustrated. The international Youth With a Mission team had been on the streets all day, and we were not getting anywhere. All two hundred of us met the next day for prayer in a rented monastery on the edge of town. We cried out to God for answers.

The crowds were there. Thousands of Argentines from all over the country had come to the finals of the world soccer play-offs, but our witnessing lacked power. Nobody was coming to Christ.

During that day of prayer and fasting, the Holy Spirit began to reveal the nature of the unseen realm over Cordoba. We realised that our timidity and weakness in proclaiming the gospel were partly due to the work of satanic forces manifesting themselves in the culture of the city.

Cordoba is a proud and beautiful city with proud and beautiful people. The population is largely of German and Italian descent, and much importance is given to position, possessions and appearance. In the midst of this fashion-conscious culture, we felt very out of place. We were Christians from over twenty nations, simply dressed, struggling with Spanish and carrying gospel literature.

The Lord responded and gave us a plan. As we prayed in small groups, the Holy Spirit revealed the same strategy to many minds. There is only one way to overcome a spirit of pride—through the humility of Jesus, through Jesus' life lived out in acts of obedience by His people. We were discerning a principality attempting to rule the city in the pride of life, so we had to confront it in an opposite spirit with a strategy of personal humility.

Here is what we did. We went downtown the next day— all two hundred of us—and formed into small groups of about thirty. We positioned ourselves all through the fashionable shopping centres and streets for pedestrians of the downtown area. Then we did it. We knelt down right there in the midst of the fashion parade, surrounded by expensive bistros, outdoor cafes and boutiques. With our foreheads to the cobblestones, we prayed for a revelation of Jesus to come to the city.

Breakthrough was immediate—breakthrough in us and breakthrough in the city. Large crowds of curious people gathered around each group.

I remember vividly how Christ strengthened me when I set aside my dignity and knelt in the street. The intimidation of the enemy was broken along with our pride. As the crowd became larger, I stood and explained through an interpreter why we had come to the city. As I lifted my voice to communicate to the people at the edge of the crowd, the boldness and compassion of the Lord filled me and I began to preach.

TAKING OUR CITIES FOR GOD

All over downtown Cordoba, Youth With a Mission workers preached to attentive audiences and a harvest of souls began. The people were so receptive that they would wait patiently in line for us personally to autograph our gospel tracts. They insisted on this unusual way of honouring us and constantly expressed gratitude for these small gospel portions. These large street meetings went on for several weeks until our departure. Large numbers came forward publicly to indicate that they had turned to Christ.

When at first we were greeted with chilling indifference, we could hear the enemy's accusation: "You are not cool enough." He followed with this temptation: "Don't demean yourself. Don't lose your dignity." He was appealing to our pride. Our response was to humble ourselves publicly.

I will never forget one evening when I was preaching in the plaza of San Martin to a large crowd and the scythe of God went through the audience. People dropped to their knees in public repentance. One woman stumbled forward weeping and, kneeling down, grasped my knees. "Can I receive Jesus right here?" she said. "Do I have to come to a church?" I assured her that she could find Christ anywhere.

Now tell me. How could a city so resistant to the gospel suddenly become such a place of harvest? The enemy holds the nations in deception and accusation. When we minister in a given city we, too, are hindered by the spirits oppressing the people, until we discern the nature of the enemy's deception and "bind the strong man" by acting in the opposite spirit.

To overcome the enemy we must resist temptation ourselves and then continue in united, travailing prayer until we sense that we have gained authority and that God has broken through. It happened in the Bible.

Remember the stories of Jericho and Ai (Josh. 6-7). The unusual strategies that God gave the children of Israel carried an intelligent purpose. Marching in silence around a wall for days on end made no sense militarily, but the people were gaining spiritual authority by the exercise of faith, obedience and self-control. That they had to march in silence is probably a clue to the nature of the unseen realm over Jericho. If they had been free to respond to the insults and mockery hurled from the walls, a spirit of contention, pride and anger may have been loosed among the people.

God's people would never overcome using the enemy's own perverse methods, so they walked in silent self-control until the victory shout, and, by God's power, the walls came tumbling down.

Ai was a stronghold with its own unique temptations. To their grief the people found that presumptuous battle without discernment and obedience to God always results in defeat.

This book focuses on the deliverance of cities and nations rather than individuals for two reasons:

• We have an abundance of good teaching on counselling and deliverance for individuals.

• We need to lift ourselves out of a self-centred spirituality—a mentality that says we are victims rather than warriors.

Fiery darts will come, but, as we raise the shield of faith, we must take up the sword of the Spirit and join with others in contending for cities and nations. Let us never forget the power that is in the Word of God. Our steps of obedience and faith contribute to a bigger victory than our own.

TWO

The Discerning of Spirits

"Casting down arguments and every high thing that exalts itself against the knowledge of God."   *2 Corinthians 10:5*

I sat on the platform with other preachers listening as Paul Yonggi Cho, pastor of Yoido Full Gospel Church, Seoul, Korea, spoke to the crowd about spiritual warfare. As he testified about a hair-raising personal confrontation with an evil spirit, the Holy Spirit turned my thoughts toward the ministry of Jesus recorded in the Gospels. Jesus seems to have been in constant confrontation with demons. He regularly discerned their presence and their work.

As I reflected on Jesus' spiritual warfare, I asked myself: when was the last time I truly exercised the gift of discernment in relation to my circumstances? I always prayerfully exercise the authority of the believer in resisting the enemy when I minister and, from time to time, I rebuke the demonic forces that I sense in a particular circumstance. But was I really seeing all that the Holy Spirit could reveal to me?

I knew that exercising the gifts of the Spirit had a lot to do with personal initiative. Our will is involved, so I asked Jesus for His view of the unseen realm in my home, my office and my ministry. "Lord, do I have blind spots?" I asked. "Are there subtle influences of demonic accusation and deception that I am totally unaware of?"

All the way home on the plane I pondered this question and turned attentively to the still, small voice of the Holy Spirit. Because I travel extensively as a Bible teacher, many people pray for me. Two intercessors in different cities had recently told me that a spirit of accusation was attempting to destroy my family and ministry. What did that really mean? How should I come against it? I can't become paranoid about demons, I thought.

Some people see deliverance as the solution for everything, when the problem may really be solved through repentance, proper management or application of some other principle. "Well, Lord,"I said, "if there is an actual demon attacking me I trust that You will show me."

The plane landed. I retrieved my baggage and flagged down my wife as she circled the Los Angeles airport in our family van. As soon as the door opened I sensed it. I felt the oppression of an evil spirit right in the van with my wife and three sons—not possessing anybody, just lurking in the background.

As we drove out of the airport I thought back over the last six months. There was definitely a pattern of criticism and misunderstanding in some of our external family relationships. I drove into a parking lot and explained to my family what I was feeling. I said that what we had gone through was more than the expected stress of a busy life. There was an insidious pattern of harassment that became clearer the more we discussed it. As the priest in my home, I joined with my wife in commanding the spirit to go from us. Immediately we sensed the departure of an evil presence.

The next day I prayed earnestly for my staff at the Los Angeles Youth With a Mission headquarters. As I prayed, a picture of the board room came into my mind. The directors meet in this room to seek the Lord and to make long–range decisions. In my mind's eye I could see a gloomy cloud hovering in a corner next to the ceiling. I understood that I was discerning a spirit of unbelief.

Yes, that's it, I thought. Every time we meet in there, everybody becomes unusually anxious about finances, even though God has proved so faithful.

I suddenly became angry—angry at a spirit that would dare to accuse our generous, faithful, heavenly Father.

During the next few days, we experienced a season of spiritual house cleaning. A spirit of confusion that had oppressed a family for months was exposed and sent into the waste places (Matt. 12:43) along with several other demons that had been practising a subtle harassment right in the middle of our Christian ministry.

It is no surprise that I was discovering demonic activity at a Youth With a Mission base. Any effective ministry is going to be the subject of satanic attack.

Satan is a religious spirit who hangs around religious leaders and institutions. He has only two weapons: to accuse and to deceive. He hurls his accusations and lies with greatest effect in the religious world.

What do we see Satan doing in the Bible? Accusing Job, deceiving Eve, accusing the saints before the throne of God and finally tempting Jesus with a kingdom without the cross. The devil built the temptations of

Jesus on a subtle accusation of the character of God the Father.

Satan is not omnipresent. Where do you think he is right now? I think he's probably trying to accuse and deceive the Christian leader who is most threatening to his kingdom. High-ranking spirits oppress Christian leaders as in the incident of delayed revelation recorded in the life story of Daniel. Daniel was kept from a God-given revelation because the territorial spirit over Persia withstood a messenger angel for twenty-one days until the angel Michael joined the fight (Dan. 10).

Most believers are well taught on the authority of the believer and the gifts of the Spirit. What I have just described is not an attempt to go over that ground again but to remind us to be vigilant.

Let me ask you the question that I asked myself that day as I listened to Pastor Cho: when was the last time you truly exercised the gift of discernment in relation to your circumstances?

Before you answer that question, remember some basics:

• The gifts of the Spirit represent the abilities of Jesus, just as the fruit of the Spirit describes the personality of Jesus.

• Jesus lives in you, the believer, and He is able to be in you and through you everything you are not.

• He is the source of our victory over sin, our wisdom, strength, love and power.

• He doesn't give us some truth. He *is* truth and He lives His life through us as we yield to His control.

One of the abilities or gifts of Jesus' Holy Spirit within us is the ability to discern or see the activity of spirits in the unseen realm (1 Cor. 12:10). We can choose to exercise this gift or neglect it even though we believe it is biblical.

Sometimes we think that the gifts of the Spirit are the special domain of "super-mature" Christians, but the truth is that they are part of God's grace expressed in order to bring all of us to maturity. You can and should stir up this gift within you. It may not be your special ministry emphasis, but discernment should not be neglected in your daily life.

But, you might ask, how do I exercise a gift? First let's look at a gift often expressed or witnessed by Christians— the gift of prophecy. Many believers have been used by the Holy Spirit to impart a special word of encouragement to other believers in a home meeting or church service. When this occurs it is not a result of the Holy Spirit's grabbing the person and forcing speech from his lips. The person usually senses the beginning of what God wants to say and voluntarily yields to the Holy Spirit in expressing that thought. He begins in faith out of love for God and His people, and as thought follows thought the prophecy moves to completion.

Exercising discernment is a similar experience in that it is an act of the will and an act of faith. It takes a child-like humility to act upon the impressions that the Holy Spirit brings us. I feel very vulnerable telling you the introductory story for this chapter because I have departed from the safe ground of the tangible and exposed to you the highly subjective experience of my inner life with God. This kind of unsophisticated vulnerability is needed if we are to see any supernatural manifestation of the Lord's power. Signs and wonders follow steps of obedience to the Master's voice.

According to the Bible our lives are lived in the midst of an invisible spiritual war. One of the most dangerous things we can do is simply to ignore this reality. We accept the Bible as true but we often live as though the battle existed on some far-off mission field, not here in our city. The fact is, there is a battle raging over your city and it is affecting you right now. Our individual blind spots and vices are usually common to the culture around us, and that culture is influenced by what the Bible calls principalities and powers (Eph. 6). In other words, you are being buffeted by the same temptations as others around you.

Another thing to note is that spiritual warfare begins at a personal level and escalates through layers of increasing difficulty—from personal and family to the realm of church life, and beyond that the collective church in the city and the national and international realms.

Have you ever thought about the battle for your immediate neighbourhood? For the last ten years I have lived in the black community in Los Angeles. My neighbours and I have common enemies. Spirits of despair, hopelessness, depression, discouragement and rejection torment this community.

Even as I write, my neighbourhood is making headlines because of gang violence and mass arrests. Much of this is explained by a history of social oppression, but we must not underestimate the spiritual implications. The Bible says that we are not fighting against flesh and blood (Eph. 6:12). The devastation of drugs and of violence stems from the destruction of the family, and the destruction of the family is accelerated in an atmosphere of despair.

What creates atmosphere? Atmosphere is a theatrical term for the collective mood of an audience during a play, but in daily life the human spirit is sensitive to many unseen things in the spiritual realm. Man is, by definition, an incarnate spirit and is sensitive to spiritual realities, including the activity of demons seeking to oppress and deceive.

Several years ago my staff and I went on a prayer walk around our neighbourhood. We stood in front of every house, rebuked Satan's work in Jesus' name and prayed for a revelation of Jesus in the life of each family. We are still praying. There is a long way to go, but social, economic and spiritual transformation is evident. There were times when demonic oppression almost crushed my soul. I received a death threat. My tyres were slashed. I was often depressed at the sight of boarded-up houses, unemployed youth, and disintegrating families, but I was determined not to run away.

Today there are at least nine Christian families in the block where I live, and there is a definite sense of the Lord's peace. The neighbourhood is no longer disintegrating. People are renovating their houses and a sense of community is being established around the Christian families.

The battle is very real. Last week a neighbour discovered a loaded pistol in my driveway just before my children came out to go to school. Drugs are sold all night several doors down at a house belonging to an alcoholic who is unchanged after years of prayer and ministry. These realities are a challenge to my faith, but I believe that as we continue in prayer the demons of hopelessness, violence and addiction will be driven from this place completely, and my neighbours will have the opportunity to receive ministry without demonic interference.

Every one of us faces demonic forces in our local environment, but as Christians we are called to a much bigger battle. We are contending for our whole generation. We are called to act locally but to think globally.

Because of massive urbanisation, it is the evangelisation of our cities that holds the key to bringing millions of people to Christ. In the next section we will discuss the modern urban environment. We will examine the context of today's great spiritual battles and try to get God's mind for our cities.

SECTION TWO

DELIVER THE DARK CITY

*"The wall of Jerusalem is also broken down,
and its gates are burned with fire. "*
Nehemiah 1:3

THREE

A Call to the City

"So I was encouraged, as the hand of the Lord my God was upon me; and I gathered chief men of Israel to go up with me."
Ezra 7:28

I was trying to help a fellow preacher sort out his life and ministry. He was one of my staff leaders. We drove through Los Angeles discussing his gifts and the options facing him.

"I don't want to minister here in LA," he said. "I don't want to raise my kids in this environment. What an armpit!" Deep within my spirit I felt a righteous anger.

"Why do you think we live here?" I said. "I'm really ashamed of you for having that attitude. Are we preachers just professional religionists looking for pleasant places to settle down? My staff and I didn't move to LA for the environmental benefits."

This dear brother eventually came to a place of repentance. He is now stationed in a foreign city with greater problems than LA, but there are millions of Christians who choose where they will live on an entirely self-centred basis. However, Christians must get Jesus' view of these cities. Cities are simply huge clusters of people, and Jesus goes where the people are. In His earthly ministry Jesus wept with compassion for the crowds of Jerusalem and moved among them in ministry.

Over one-half of the world's population lives in urban centres. In developed nations like the United States, the percentage of urban dwellers is much higher. In California, for example, 91 percent of the population lives in cities.

My city, Los Angeles, is crowded, expensive, violent and polluted. I would rather raise my children in rural isolation or suburban convenience, but Jesus has called me here. Jesus has always been attracted to the dark places. "But where sin abounded, grace abounded much more" (Rom. 5:20).

By the year 2010, three out of every four people on earth will live in cities, which means that cities must become the prime target of the missionary. Today's church is much more comfortable sending missionaries from suburban churches to the rural villages of Africa or Central America. Too many Christians feel alienated by the city and see it only as a dark and evil place to be avoided, but this is not God's attitude. Consider His words to the Jews held captive in pagan Babylon. "And seek the peace of the city where I have caused you to be carried away captive, and pray to the Lord for it; for in its peace you will have peace" (Jer. 29:7).

More than half of the people in the United States live in 6 percent of the land area. Translated, that means eighty-eight million people live in the forty-four largest metropolitan areas. The larger cities are filled with a multiplicity of ethnic peoples who have turned the

United States into one of the major mission fields of the world. With four and a half million Hispanics, Los Angeles is now the second largest Hispanic city. It is also the second largest Chinese city outside Asia and the second largest Japanese city outside Japan. The list goes on. It is the largest Korean city outside Korea, the largest Vietnamese city outside Vietnam and the largest Philippine city outside the Philippines.

A century ago London was the world's only supercity, but now forty-two cities of the world have a population surpassing four million. Most of these cities are either Asian or Islamic. When we add those that are Marxist we get some idea of the challenge Christians face in world evangelisation.

It's time for us to put aside our fear and self-interest and to take bold action. I recently heard about a newly appointed pastor to a comfortable middle-class church in the suburbs of Fort Worth, Texas. He proposed that the expensive church property be sold and that the congregation move its ministries to the inner city. He's no longer with that church. He didn't succeed, but his is the kind of radical idea I think is needed.

We must have a new vision of Christian service. The mission field has always had a romance to it, with visions of primitive tribes and palm trees in the setting sun. We need to plant another dream in the hearts of our young pioneers. We must fill their minds with a more realistic and compelling picture.

Our new vision of Christian missions must focus on cities. If we want to bring nations to Christ, we must win their cities. Here's the reason: there was a time prior to the rise of modern nationalism when the civilised world consisted of a cluster of city-states like Venice or Luxembourg. Today, apart from Hong Kong, Singapore, Luxembourg, which still survives, and a few others, the world consists of entities we call nations, which often embrace more than one world-class city within national borders.

In reality a nation is a geographical and political alliance among its major cities. A nation is a sum of its cities. The cities are the mind and heart of the nation, the place where the national myth is largely enshrined. The land between the cities is sparsely populated, serving to sustain the continuing life of the city. This includes agriculture, energy and some remote artistic communities that exist only by serving the urban market. More importantly, political power issues from and resides in those who represent the people of the city.

As we dream of discipling nations, we must firmly grasp the reality of these nations. That means the gospel must transform the spiritual, philosophical and physical life of a nation's cities. If it does anything less, we have failed to win the battle, no matter how magnificent our national Christian organisations may appear to be.

The early days of the Salvation Army are a graphic example of the power of the gospel transforming the life of the city. General Booth and his followers had clearly identified the prevailing satanic bondages of their day (alcoholism and prostitution), and they employed city-wide strategies which resulted in city-wide victories.

Let's renew our determination to disciple the nations, but let's do it with a radical and realistic vision. Let's lift up Christ's banner in the dirtiest, darkest places. Let's take on the giant of the impersonal, looming city.

When I first arrived in Los Angeles, I felt engulfed by the vastness of the city. I felt small and irrelevant. How could anyone have an impact on a city so big, so impersonal and so diverse? I couldn't even see the people; they were inside cars and buildings. The city seemed sterile. Impenetrable.

Only prayer changed my perspective. I began to have the mind of Christ, the attitude and perspective of Jesus. I actually wept over my city. Now I feel God's compassion for the people of the city. I love my city.

And I've seen it change— really change for the better.

We have a gift. We have spiritual authority. We have experienced deliverance. We know God's power. We can stand before God for the city and know that He will respond.

> Arise, shine,
> For your light has come!
> And the glory of the Lord is risen upon you.
> For behold, the darkness shall cover the earth,
> And deep darkness the people;
> But the Lord will arise over you,
> And His glory will be seen upon you.
> The Gentiles shall come to your light,
> And kings to the brightness of your rising
> (Is. 60:1-3).

FOUR

Cities: A Blessing or a Curse?

"Where there is no vision, the people perish."   *Proverbs 29:18, KJV*

Many Christians think cities are by nature evil places. If they were asked, they would say the city is a curse, not a blessing. However, that is not God's view. After all, the human story begins in a garden and ends in a city.

I believe God intends the city to be a place of shelter, a place of communion and a place of personal liberation as its citizens practise a division of labour according to their own unique gifts. I believe our cities have the mark of God's sovereign purpose upon them. Our cities contain what I call a redemptive gift.

A city is a human institution, and like all institutions it develops a creaturehood or personality that is greater than the sum of its parts. Each metropolis has unique characteristics when compared with other cities.

For example, New York City is a hub of trade and a centre for world leadership. But it is more than that—it symbolises a life-style dream. The dream of wealth and power draws people to New York, and they are seduced by the success-fantasy for which New York has become a giant metaphor.

Today ruthlessness and despair haunt Manhattan, and most Christians see only the negative influence of the city, but how does God see New York? Does He have a plan, a purpose for the city? Originally it was the gateway of hope to the land of liberty. These are strong and godly qualities that suggest God's redemptive purpose for this great urban centre.

Think about the personality of your city. Noted historian Arnold Toynbee, in his introduction to the book *Cities of Destiny*, defines the city as follows: "In order to become a city, it would have to evolve at least the rudiments of a soul. This is perhaps the essence of cityhood."

As a Christian intercessor, I find Toynbee's observation very interesting. Does a city have a "soul", as he puts it? Any astute observer can see that certain cities seem to embody a central dream, and there is usually both a good and evil side to that dream.

I believe God has participated in the creation of our cities both in forming their personality and in stationing high–ranking guardian angels over each one. For example, the angel Michael is referred to as the "great prince" standing watch over Israel (Dan. 12:1), and then there is the experience of Elisha's servant recorded in 2 Kings 6:16-17:

> So he answered, "Do not fear, for those who are with us are more than those who are with them." And Elisha prayed, and said, "Lord, I pray, open his eyes that he

> may see." Then the Lord opened the eyes of
> the young man, and he saw. And behold, the
> mountain was full of horses and chariots of
> fire all around Elisha.

If our eyes were opened in like manner, what would
we see? The Greek word *angelos* in the New Testament
means "messenger". What message would an angel of
the Lord bring concerning your city? Would God reveal
a divine purpose? On the other hand, Satan will do
anything in his power to accuse your city, to malign its
redemptive gift.

Let me give you an example. A citizen of Amsterdam
has a right to be proud of the centuries-old tradition of
hospitality and tolerance that mark the culture of that
city. Amsterdam is a genuine city of refuge, like world-
famous Geneva or some of the cities of the Levites listed
in the Old Testament.

Today, however, it's a city known for tolerating open
drug sales and legal prostitution. This is plainly a
perversion of a gift. Amsterdam needs a fresh picture of
itself functioning in righteousness, an identity rooted in
the prophetic vision of its Christian community. Indeed
God has begun to raise up dynamic ministries in this,
one of Europe's darkest cities.

Determining your city's redemptive gift is even more
important than discerning the nature of evil
principalities. Principalities rule through perverting the
gift of a city in the same way as an individual's gift is
turned to the enemy's use through sin.

Satan is not a creator. He cannot originate anything.
He can only turn created things and people to his own
purposes. It is easy to identify the motivational gifts of
unsaved individuals and to see what their ministry
would be if they were saved and filled with the Holy
Spirit.

For example, John Lennon would have been a
minstrel prophet like King David, and rock guitarist

Jimi Hendrix could have become an excellent worship leader.

I once set out to convert the manager of a local porno store. We had breakfast together on Wednesday mornings for several weeks. He believed everything I had to say about Jesus, but he would not take the final step of committing himself to follow the Lord.

One morning I said, "Ron, you're a tough guy on the outside, but inside you're soft. You have what the Bible calls a gift of mercy. If you would allow Jesus to take over, you would become the kind of person to whom others would come for healing and comfort." For the first time he looked at me with real hope in his eyes, and that was the day he made Jesus his Lord.

Applying this principle to cities, we see the tragic example of the city of Jerusalem. Mount Zion is ordained by God to be a city of peace and praise. Instead, it has become a place of conflict where God's character is continuously misrepresented through religious controversy.

In spite of the present torment of Jerusalem, we still find it easy to identify God's redemptive purpose for that city. Why? Because the Bible reveals many prophetic statements concerning Jerusalem's destiny. God's people were agents of revelation, speaking out God's intention.

This principle is true today. Where will destiny and purpose for your city be revealed except through the prophetic gift within God's church? It is the goodness of God that leads to repentance. We cannot call a city to repentance without calling it to ongoing purpose. The gospel awakens the gift. "Where there is no vision, the people perish" (Prov. 29:18, KJV).

It is a psychological principle that he who gives the greatest hope gains the greatest authority. We see this principle used by politicians at election time. We Christians must use it to help restore our cities to God's purpose.

The gospel is good news, stirring hope in a God who never disappoints us. Christians have denounced the city too long. It's time we stood at the centre of urban culture speaking to our city of positive possibilities.

Psalm 48 embodies the appreciation of God's people for Jerusalem and shows what care God takes in locating our cities:

> Great is the Lord, and greatly to be praised.
> In the city of our God,
> In His holy mountain.
> Beautiful in elevation,
> The joy of the whole earth,
> Is Mount Zion on the sides of the north,
> The city of the great King (Ps. 48:1-2).

Jerusalem's placement was no coincidence and neither is the location of your city.

When I am travelling and preaching, one of the first questions I ask upon arrival is, "Why is this town here?" I am often treated to a baffled look and a shrug of the shoulders.

There is always a reason, and that reason usually stems from the geography of the location, such as a mountain pass, rich soil, mineral wealth, a river crossing or a natural port.

A few years ago my oldest son, David, was given a school assignment on the geography of California. We worked together making a large clay model of the topography of the whole state. As my fingers pressed up the mountain ranges and pushed down the valleys, I began to marvel at the geographic design of the area.

I was struck by the fact that the coastal range was just the right height to let moisture pass over until meeting the ramparts of the high Sierras, where the clouds are forced to dump their moisture in the form of winter snow. This winter snow becomes a giant storehouse for the irrigation systems in the vast agricultural plain of

43

the San Joaquin Valley.

This is no accident. The earth has been lovingly crafted as a habitation for people. God anticipated the development of your city. He marked out a place for it.

When we acknowledge the placement of our cities as a function of God's sovereignty, we begin to see things we have never seen before. I recently spoke to a pastor's gathering in Omaha, Nebraska, and was excited to learn that they had a clear sense of destiny for their city.

Omaha was once the place where pioneering wagon trains were provisioned for the arduous trail into the western wilderness. "We believe that we are still to equip the pioneers," one pastor told me. "This time it is to support world-wide missionary work." Now that's a vision worth living for.

I believe Salt Lake City has a similar gift, but the enemy has perverted it through false religion. The key to reaching the cities of Utah is to communicate a vision of missions more comprehensive and compassionate than the destiny that Mormonism now offers to the young people of that state.

When I look at my own city, Los Angeles, I have to hold two truths in tension. On one hand, it is a technological tower of Babel, polluting the world with its communications and entertainment industry. On the other hand, it is a city with a gift in communications. Los Angeles is a city blessed by God with certain resources that can either be perverted or converted.

Even the name of the city speaks of its destiny. Los Angeles is Spanish for "The Angels". As we have already learned, *angelos* in Greek means "messenger". God wants LA to be a messenger, communicating the good news in the midst of an end time harvest.

Indeed, this plan of God has already enjoyed success several times in history: in 1906 through the Azusa Street revival; in 1949 through an evangelical renewal leading to the birth of such groups as Campus Crusade for Christ and the launching of the Billy Graham crusades as a national ministry; in 1972 with the beginning of the Jesus movement.

Today the city is torn by violence, and it pumps pornography into the minds of millions. However, LA is also a city filled with dynamic Christian ministries reaching the whole world. The church here is not asleep. We are expecting God to demonstrate His mighty power in our city. Once during the writing of this book, I met with twelve hundred other pastors and leaders in a day of prayer, called for by our senior churchmen.

God is sovereignly rebuilding the walls of our city, starting with the leadership of His churches. I believe that as we continue to meet, God will pour out revelation concerning His redemptive plans for the city. It was to the Jews living in the wicked city of Babylon that God spoke these words, "For I know the thoughts that I think toward you, says the Lord, thoughts of peace and not of evil, to give you a future and a hope" (Jer. 29:11).

God is always up to something. What is He planning for your city?

FIVE

Ministering in the City of the Future

"Issachar. . .had understanding of the times, to know what Israel ought to do. "
1 Chronicles 12:32

Twenty years ago Alvin Toffler wrote a book titled *Future Shock*, predicting the rapid transformation of our modern cities into what he called the "superindustrial society". That future is now. He portrayed the modern urbanite as a person shell-shocked by the pace of change. No one is more affected by this than the pastor of a local church and his leadership team.

In order to talk about new strategies for ministry, we need to examine the nature of today's cities and how they have developed.

First of all, the physical geography of the city has radically changed. The villages of the past had a commerce limited to the horse and cart. In most countries even the largest cities had no more than a hundred thousand people until the seventeenth century when the scientific revolution began to have its impact.

In the nineteenth century the first railway systems led to rapid expansion of the city, but it still retained its dominant centre. In the 1960s, the downtown areas became so congested and unattractive that urban growth spread to a cluster of smaller city centres within the greater metropolitan areas. Sociologists have had to invent a whole new vocabulary to describe the changing city. From *village* to *city* to *dynapolis* to *metropolis* to *dynametropolis* to *megalopolis* and presently *dynamegalopolis*.

The cities of the past were built to human scale. With few exceptions a man could walk from the wall to the centre in less than fifteen minutes. In today's cities, the dimensions have become nonhuman. In spite of the presence of occasional green belts, to the casual observer it may be difficult to know where Washington, D.C., ends and Baltimore begins, even though some twenty miles of highway separate the old city centres.

Los Angeles is already an unofficial supercity sprawling over one hundred miles with a population larger than all states in the United States except California, New York and Texas. Cities used to be contained by counties. Now the Los Angeles metroplex includes five different counties.

Such a city has not just one centre but many centres, not just one authority but many authorities; because of its scale and diversity it has become very difficult for us humans to comprehend. This is one reason why city governments are so ineffective. The city is out of control and demonstrates this through irrational situations. Consider these facts:

• Two-thirds of the central, four square miles of Los Angeles have been taken over by highways and parking, destroying a great deal of the area serviced.

• As our transport machines get faster we spend more and more time travelling to the centre of our city.

• We solve the problem of downtown blight through urban renewal programmes but create a new even larger ring of problems around the previous centre.

It is a vicious circle.

The suburbs that people escaped to in the 1960s and 1970s have become cities themselves and sometimes contain worse problems than the original city centre. People no longer commute in one direction. They traverse several different communities to shop or be entertained. Corporate headquarters and new industrial parks are now located many miles from downtown and have fused together in new urban masses.

By 1960 the number of Americans living and working in the suburbs was greater than those commuting to work in the cities. The suburbs grew so rapidly that they soon qualified as urban areas with the accompanying problems of congestion, pollution, blight and crime.

How has all this impacted humankind socially? The city is supposedly developed for our benefit. The city is a giant architectural machine commissioned to shelter, transport, empower and enrich its inhabitants; yet individual men and women increasingly feel like victims of their own creation.

Here are twelve factors that contribute to the disorientation of modern city dwellers:

1) Authority is distant and impersonal. *They feel powerless.*
2) The great majority of people are total strangers to the individual. *They feel alone.*
3) Culture, race and language are so diverse that

these factors are no longer a basis for security or identity. *They feel vulnerable.*

4) Superimposed on the diversity is a universal commercial culture of identical chain restaurants, businesses, malls, theatres and architecture, producing a nationwide urban uniformity that dwarfs regional culture. *They feel lost.*

5) Urban people have their senses continually bombarded by powerful media. *They feel controlled.*

6) Functional specialisation is to the point where family members lead completely different lives in different environments with different schedules. Family proximity comes only as the result of conscious effort. *They feel rejected.*

7) So many options are available in life-styles, products and entertainments that the promise of happiness through affluence has been swallowed up in anxiety over decision making. *They feel bewildered.*

8) An information overload has dulled the appetite for true understanding. *They feel foolish.*

9) The rapid pace of change in vocations and housing has undermined all forms of covenantal relationship. Nearly all friendships are short-term. *They feel insecure.*

10) They are surrounded by relentless activity day and night, suggesting that others are busy achieving wealth and success. It is difficult to rest. *They feel stress and anxiety.*

11) The marketplace values them only for their skills and their labour; if they fail they are rejected like cast-off machinery. *They feel used.*

12) Public values are reduced to the promotion of production and consumption. All other values are considered private. *They feel void of meaning.*

Because of the disorientation they experience, urban dwellers are extremely vulnerable to both sweeping revival and mass deception through some false hope. The city dweller is often an idolater. The city intensifies everything, and this includes devotion to false gods.

To practise idolatry is to substitute something man-made for God. All three persons of the trinity have their function imitated by idols:

• The counterfeit of the work of the Holy Spirit is false religion.

• The Son is replaced in the form of human heroes and deliverers.

• The Father is replaced by institutions.

From the Father we receive identity, security, provision, protection and direction. The moment we turn to an institution as the prime object of our faith, we have become an idolater.

The city is a cluster of overlapping institutions. All institutions have a servant function. They must provide some form of service in order to survive. The army, the school, the hospital, the national government and the city all represent the division of labour at a corporate level. Satan seeks to rule by influencing these institutions, especially through the church, arts and entertainment, and commerce. He seeks not only to demonise the atmosphere of these institutions but to mark them with his own characteristics, to make them into an extension of his kingdom.

God is not anti-institutional; it is His own nature within us that causes us to build mechanisms with the potential to bless.

We need to look at institutions as containers filled with people, people who need to be evangelised. True, many institutions have a morally questionable purpose and need to be reformed, such as abortion clinics, but most institutions are morally neutral. It is the character of the people that needs to be changed. Only the transforming power of the gospel can do that.

This leads us back to the promise of revival. We know what revival looked like at the turn of the century in New England or Wales. We even have reports of revival today in some Asian and Latin American countries, but what would revival look like in the superindustrial cities of the information age? I believe that our old pictures of revival are an encouragement, but I also believe that they can become one of the greatest hindrances to our faith. Why? Because the villages that Charles Finney and Evan Roberts described bear no resemblance to our modern cities.

I once had the privilege of being taught by one of the world's greatest revival historians. I asked him about the validity of the Jesus movement in 1972-1974. He discounted it as a true revival saying that the whole society was not transformed as in the days of classic historic revival.

Something about his answer disturbed my spirit, so I began to think deeply about my own generation and its urban environment.

Originally people clustered in fortress cities for protection. But, in the modern city, people cluster together to benefit from the principle of specialisation within the division of labour. People are able to excel in the job that suits them best and in turn be served by others who are expert in their fields.

The city then becomes a cluster of villages or subcultures each serving the other. These are not like the traditional rural villages that have a common geography, authority and purpose which are easily understood. The urban village is a village of communication that is structured around specialised vocations.

Think of the haulage industry as an example. It has a

common purpose (to transport goods), a common authority (industry law and contracts), and a common geography (motorways, streets and warehouses). Lorry drivers even have their own language.

It is easy to identify a communication village such as an ethnic neighbourhood or college campus, but urban dwellers are usually members of less obvious subcultures that give definition to their lives. An example would be the salesman on used-car row relating to the vocational village of dealers and mechanics.

Think of revival hitting the modern city. The Spirit of God moves through people as they communicate one with another. The people we communicate with are those in our vocational village and those to whom we relate because of special interests or needs. We are commuters.

Just like our ancestors, we live and die having related to about thirty people, but those people are usually not our neighbours. Proximity has little to do with relationship. It is easier for me to conduct a relationship with my friend Nick in New York City by telephone than it is for me to get out of my chair, walk down the street and befriend my neighbour four doors down.

Revival will not spread from house to house in the dormitory suburbs of the modern city. Yet we are burdened with that very expectation because of the mental images we carry from the past.

I believe the Jesus movement was a genuine awakening and we can learn from it. It represented the first example of revival in the modern city. In 1972 there was a sovereign move of God's Spirit on a "communication village" layered laterally throughout Western urban culture. This village consisted of counterculture youth—the Woodstock generation.

This was the first generation to live in a global village. Because of mass media they not only consumed the same soft drinks but joined in a common philosophy and life-style. From Durban, South Africa, to Perth, Australia, kids experienced Beatle-mania and the slide into drugs and Eastern mysticism.

The situation was desperate. The generation of the sixties became addicted, demonised, promiscuous and negative toward the gospel. Then a strange thing happened. In odd locations like Germantown, Pennsylvania, and Huntington Beach, California, counterculture youth began showing up in church with a testimony of having met Jesus.

This was not the product of any organisation or of any man but it did parallel the charismatic renewal of the late sixties and early seventies. During the renewal, thousands of heartbroken parents cried out to God for their devastated children, and the result was the worldwide ingathering known as the Jesus movement.

In 1973 I was in Canada, but far away in New Zealand almost all of my old heathen friends were saved. Most Americans are unaware of the truly worldwide nature of the Jesus movement. No matter where they lived, if their lifestyle was drugs, sex and rock 'n' roll in 1972, thousands had a powerful revelation of Jesus.

This example gives me great hope. When I look at our churches, I see a missing generation. Where are the youth? The children of the sixties are the parents of today's teenagers, children who have had no powerful revelation of Jesus in their generation.

When I look at my city, the youth appear to be as devastated as they did in the sixties. This time it's crack and gang violence. The situation appears hopeless, but God is still the God of revival. God still comes in mercy to the undeserving and the deceived when we intercede on their behalf.

When we pray we need to pray for revival in any form that God might want to bring it. An awakening could spread through a specific subculture, such as the people involved in real estate sales and construction. Can you picture that? An anointed imagination is the eye of faith. Can you see that influential real estate man getting saved and a harvest taking place concentrated in one industry? When David toppled Goliath, a lot of Philistines rolled over. God can still work that way today.

The average Christian, overwhelmed by the sheer size of the city and its problems, prays for the city with very low expectations. However, behind the walls and rooftops, behind the storefronts and landscaping, individual people live their lives as part of small villages of communication.

In the place of prayer we will receive from God a specific strategy of spiritual warfare and a specific strategy of evangelism. After all, the city is tiny, temporary and fragile when seen from the throne of God.

"Behold, the nations are as a drop in a bucket, and are counted as the small dust on the balance; look, He lifts up the isles as a very little thing" (Is. 40:15).

SIX

Revival or Judgment What Will It Be?

"Will you not revive us again, that Your people may rejoice in You?"

Psalm 85:6

When my friend Floyd finished preaching and called for repentance, I was the first to my feet. During the message I had seen myself clearly and I was ashamed. I publicly confessed my sin that day and asked the others at the conference for prayer.

What was my sin? Embezzlement, adultery? No, the Holy Spirit was convicting me of the sin of unbelief. In that stark moment of honesty I realised that I really had low expectations of what God would do in my city.

What do you expect God to do in your city? Or, to put it another way, who is your God? Is He the God of the Bible? Your God is only as big as what you expect of Him in space and time. What do you expect Him to do here on earth in this generation? Don't tell me about the God of your theology. It's easy to say that He's all-powerful, but do you expect Him to do powerful things here and now?

The God of the Bible is the God who sweeps in like a mighty rushing wind. He answers by fire. He is the God of great awakenings and generation-wide revivals.

The time of my repentance came not long after God used me and others to lead a great city-wide outreach during the 1984 Summer Olympics in Los Angeles. We had experienced a touch of revival at that time, but now I was seeing myself two years later as just a busy religious executive struggling to manage the results of a past success. I had lost sight of the big picture. I no longer felt the sense of God's mighty presence brooding over the city.

I looked back at the man I had been during that outreach. I remembered what it had been like to weep and to pray and to allow God to fill my heart with a city-wide vision.

As I repented of my unbelief and its root of pride, God came in mercy and began to fill my heart with a gift of faith for the future, a renewed faith for revival in America's cities.

We as believers hold the fate of our cities in our hands. Revival or judgment—what will it be?

Strangely enough, the answer may be both. If we look to church history, we see that judgment and revival often happen at the same time. Think of John Wycliffe, the "Morning Star of the Reformation" (1330-1384). At the same time as he was disseminating his new English translation of the Bible, over one-third of the English population died of the black death. The followers of Wycliffe, known as Lollards, affirmed obedience to the Word of God and brought to the English church such a wave of repentance from dead works that the Lollards became a threat to the religious establishment and were severely persecuted.

What will happen in the end times? Some say a great falling away, while others predict a worldwide revival. Again the answer is both. The Bible predicts a great polarisation of darkness and light at the end of the age. Satan will unmask his kingdom and intensify his efforts. There will be no illusion of middle ground. On the other hand the Spirit of God will be poured out on the earth and an unparalleled harvest will be gathered into His kingdom.

Is this the last generation? I don't know, but I do know that we are in grave danger of severe judgment. God is a God of mercy and grace, but He is also a holy God who hates the suffering caused by wicked people. God judges a city or a nation only when people have repeatedly rejected His message and warning. But judgment is His last resort.

Take a look at America. The statistics are horrifying.

• We have killed twenty million unborn babies in the last fifteen years—one every twenty seconds, four thousand children a day.

• Parental affection for children has eroded to the point where 20,860 babies and toddlers were simply abandoned nationwide in 1986. This statistic has tripled in only ten years, and child abuse has multiplied twenty times over.

• Pornography is a $32 billion business.

• Illegal drug sales are estimated to top $20 billion.

• Homosexuality is now an accepted life-style, and adultery is casually regarded as being "sexually active" or having "multiple partners".

Considering the fact that God judges a nation according to its knowledge of the truth, the United

States is in deep trouble. We are beginning to make God our enemy. "Then He began to upbraid the cities in which most of His mighty works had been done, because they did not repent....'But I say to you that it shall be more tolerable for the land of Sodom in the day of judgment than for you' " (Matt. 11:20,24). What nation has been exposed to the truth of the gospel more than the United States?

Already we are beginning to see God's protective hand lifting. There has begun a pattern of plagues, natural disasters, economic upheavals and destructive changes in the weather. We must take these warnings seriously.

In 1983 my spirit became increasingly grieved over the wickedness of Los Angeles. Day after day I opened the Bible to passages describing impending judgment. It seemed as though God had suddenly edited out the promise of blessing. I remember meditating on Leviticus 26:31 with a distinct sense that this was what God was actually saying about my city: "I will lay your cities waste and bring your sanctuaries to desolation."

I felt the need to join with other intercessors and was not surprised to find that all over the city people of prayer had received warnings of impending disaster. I remember one prayer meeting in particular. I was praying with my mother, Joy Dawson, and a pastor friend of ours named Dan Sneed. As we waited before the Lord, Scripture references came to mind, mostly unfamiliar passages. When we looked them up, they were all pronouncements of severe judgment.

We cried out to God for mercy on the city, but we received no promise of mercy that day. This season of travail for mercy lasted until the last day of the Olympic outreach in the summer of 1984. Let me describe that day.

At 6:00 a.m. I was awakened by a call from Jack Hayford, the pastor of one of our city's most vital churches. "John, I am calling our church to pray with special urgency today," he said. He was sensing, like many others, that we could only avert some serious catastrophe in the city through fervent prayer.

Outside there was no sign of impending calamity. The sun was shining on a city decorated with thousands of Olympic banners. The world had just witnessed a showcase of American hospitality and management expertise.

In my heart I knew we needed to pray as never before. I began to make calls.

At a rally in a city park, the Youth With a Mission workers were scheduled that day to report on their evangelism. We had mobilised eleven thousand people for personal evangelism during the Olympics. Over six thousand of these were Youth With a Mission workers from around the world.

I called Loren Cunningham, the director of YWAM. He and his staff turned their rally into a giant outdoor prayer meeting for the city.

In an unforgettable scene, Christians from over thirty countries lifted their voices in many languages, interceding for our city. They were seated on the grass in small groups all over the park, eyes closed, lifting their voices in earnest prayer.

Not until 4:30 that afternoon did that season of travail begin to change. Simultaneously, many prayer groups began to receive prophetic words and portions of Scripture describing God's protection and God's mercy.

I believe that in that summer of 1984 something terrible was about to happen in Los Angeles and that it was averted through the repentance, obedience and earnest prayer of thousands of Christians across the city. God is still looking for people who will stand in the gap before Him, as described in this tragic passage from the book of Ezekiel.

"The people of the land have used oppres–

sions, committed robbery, and mistreated the poor and needy; and they wrongfully oppress the stranger.

"So I sought for a man among them who would make a wall, and stand in the gap before Me on behalf of the land, that I should not destroy it; but I found no one.

"Therefore I have poured out my indignation on them; I have consumed them with the fire of My wrath; and I have recompensed their deeds on their own heads," says the Lord God.

(Ezek. 22:29-31)

There is a point when God will irrevocably destroy a rebellious city. "But they mocked the messengers of God, despised His words, and scoffed at His prophets, until the wrath of the Lord arose against His people, *till there was no remedy*" (2 Chr. 36:16, italics mine).

But God is usually using judgment as a form of loving discipline. The prophet Isaiah speaks of judgment followed by revival.

> On the land of my people will come up
> thorns and briers.
> Yes, on all the happy homes in the joyous
> city;
> Because the palaces will be forsaken.
> The bustling city will be deserted.
> The forts and towers will become lairs
> forever,
> A joy of wild donkeys, a pasture of
> flocks—
> *Until the Spirit is poured upon us from on
> high,*
> And the wilderness becomes a fruitful
> field,

And the fruitful field is counted as a
   forest.
(Is. 32:13-15, italics mine)

People of faith are promised protection during times of judgment on a wicked city, as illustrated by the protection of Rahab when Jericho was destroyed. However, it is important to understand that God comes among His people as a refiner's fire exposing and judging sin in answer to our prayers for revival. "For the time has come for judgment to begin at the house of God..." (1 Pet. 4:17).

We are entering into troubling times. God is pruning and purifying the leadership of His church, in order to prepare us for a harvest, the likes of which the world has never seen—a harvest gathered during a time when men's systems will fail them, a time of fear, anger and turbulence.

As we see the explosive growth of huge cities, we could also see disasters unmatched in human history. The densely populated high-rise buildings of Mexico City have already demonstrated the enormous death toll of an urban earthquake. The destruction of Hiroshima and Nagasaki has shown us the vulnerability of the city in modern war. But there is also a positive side to the emergence of supercities.

The emergence of a worldwide urban culture is setting the stage for the world's first truly global awakening. From China to Brazil, cities are becoming more and more uniform in culture. People wear Western clothes, watch television and acquire goods from stores. Rationality imposes a uniform architecture worldwide, and people are linked by international financial and entertainment networks. Entertainment in the form of films, rock music and television is discipling the youth of the world into a universal urban culture. In the cities of Africa, the children can imitate the dance steps of Michael Jackson. This global unification of mission fields, especially among youth, represents a significant new development.

In the 1940s we had a few worldwide commercial products like Coca Cola, but in the 1960s it was human personalities that became universally known. The Beatles boasted that they were more popular than Jesus Christ, and unfortunately that may have been true.

English as a second language is spoken by the elite of most world-class cities, thus creating the potential for the rapid spread of a product or an idea. English is used by as many as one billion people, yet only 360 million speak it as a mother tongue.

The linguistic streams are flowing into English, enriching its vocabulary and making it a language that has an irreversible momentum regardless of the decline of British and American power.

The statistics are astonishing. The Oxford English Dictionary lists half a million words, yet another half million technical terms remain uncatalogued. For comparison, French has fewer than one hundred thousand words.

For a global awakening to occur, it is imperative that we experience revival in the English-speaking world, particularly in the United States. The media of American are polluting the earth to the point where Iranian Muslims denounce her as the Great Satan.

Could American media and technology be turned to bless instead of curse? That's an important question. But revival in the English-speaking world could rapidly disseminate the gospel to the great cities even without access to media.

Besides English, there are thirteen great trade languages, such as Russian and Portuguese, which occupy linguistic territories, and under them we find the languages of less numeric people and tribes. The trend is toward less and less linguistic isolation.

It is time to exercise worldwide faith, to pray worldwide prayers and to expect a worldwide outpouring of God's Spirit. More than half the people who have ever lived are now alive. The world population is climbing past five billion. If we don't have an awakening in this generation, more people will go to an eternity without Christ than in all the past generations put together. I can't see God allowing that to happen. Business-as-usual is not good enough; there is not enough time.

What we must have is a sovereign outpouring of the Holy Spirit on God's people, followed by a great awakening among the lost. King David's last recorded prayer is a heart cry for a worldwide revelation of God's glory: "...and let the whole earth be filled with His glory. Amen and Amen. The prayers of David the son of Jesse are ended" (Ps. 72:19-20).

Is it possible that there will come a time soon when the whole earth will be filled with His glory? I believe that the prayers of David and the saints of many generations will be answered as the Great Commission is completed in the midst of an end-time outpouring of God's Spirit that will surpass all others.

The universal urban culture, the great trade languages and the international communication and transport systems are setting the stage for a revelation of Jesus that will affect every person on earth. The fact that the Bible predicts that the spirit of antichrist will exploit these same phenomena is not our prime concern. Our priority is the completion of the Great Commission and the return of our King.

> Rain down, you heavens, from above,
> And let the skies pour down righteousness;
> Let the earth open, let them bring forth
>   salvation;
> And let righteousness spring up together.
> I, the Lord, have created it (Is. 45:8).

In true revival the Holy Spirit is poured out in

awesome power. The Hebrew word for *spirit* is *ruach* which comes from the root meaning "to breathe out violently, implying explosive force or energy". On the day of Pentecost, timid believers were transformed into bold evangelists who feared God more than people, and the gospel was preached with power resulting in a great harvest.

The Old Testament prophets foresaw the empowering that would come to the followers of Jesus, the Messiah.

> And it shall come to pass afterward
> That I will pour out My Spirit on all flesh;
> Your sons and your daughters shall
>   prophesy,
> Your old men shall dream dreams,
> Your young men shall see visions;
> And also on My menservants and on My
>   maidservants
> I will pour out My Spirit in those days.
> And I will show wonders in the heavens
>   and in the earth:
> Blood and fire and pillars of smoke.
> The sun shall be turned into darkness,
> And the moon into blood,
> Before the coming of the great and terrible
>   day of the Lord.
> And it shall come to pass
> That whoever calls on the name of the
>   Lord
> Shall be saved (Joel 2:28-32).

Note the categories that are anointed for ministry during revival: sons and daughters, old men and young men, menservants and maidservants. We will be surprised at whom the Holy Spirit anoints for leadership in the coming revival. I believe that strong leadership will be provided by Korean, black and

American Indian Christians and that prophets and evangelists will emerge who are of junior high school age or younger.

Revival will hammer into our religious pride and complacency. For that reason the religious establishment will be tempted to resist the wind of God's Spirit and to criticise those involved. To deliver us from this temptation, God is presently shaking the leadership that emerged during the evangelical upsurge of the 1950s, and He is disciplining the leadership that emerged from the charismatic renewal and the Jesus movement of the seventies.

Do not lose hope in this present season of pruning in the vineyard. Look up and see God almighty. This work of chastisement is to prepare us for the power. Like the early church we are to gather in unity, humility and repentance in an upper room experience, waiting for the Spirit to be poured out.

Our prayer should be Isaiah 64:1-3:

> Oh, that You would rend the heavens!
> That You would come down!
> That the mountains might shake at Your
>   presence—
> As fire burns brushwood,
> As fire causes water to boil—
> To make Your name known to Your
>   adversaries,
> That the nations may tremble at Your
>   presence!
> When You did awesome things for which
>   we did not look.

SEVEN

The City at Harvest Time

*"But the people who know their God shall
be strong, and carry out great exploits. "*
Daniel 11:32

We have worked our way up to this important
tactical question: do we wait for the next revival or do
we go into action now? Obviously, we are never to
draw back from evangelisation, for we were born to
reproduce when we were born again. Evangelism must
be our life-style.

Over the years I have been part of many outreaches
to cities all over the world. I remember going door to
door in the tenements of Paris with a small team in
1971. With 1,200 others I witnessed on the streets of
Munich in 1972. I have coordinated outreaches to small
American towns and large Latin American cities. I have
joined with others in many different strategies and

methods. At one time I was part of the executive team for the Los Angeles Billy Graham Crusade, while at the same time pioneering inner-city ministries to runaways, refugees and children. In all these endeavours I have learned the central importance of prayer and spiritual warfare.

Unless you understand biblical warfare you will be frustrated, angry, confused and ineffective in your ministry to the city. You may be attempting to coordinate Christian concerts, pioneer a church or reach businessmen. The principle is still the same: we need to bind the strong man and gain a place of authority over Satan before we will see the full fruit of our labours.

Jesus said, "But if I cast out demons by the Spirit of God, surely the kingdom of God has come upon you. Or else how can one enter a strong man's house and plunder his goods, unless he first binds the strong man? And then he will plunder his house" (Matt. 12:28-29).

If we are not using our biblical spiritual weapons, we are failing the people we are attempting to serve. One of my earliest experiences with the power of prayer occurred when I was preaching in Canadian high schools in the winter of 1973. In each city I would gain access to the campus through the Christian club, and we would then use a number of creative ways to draw a crowd and preach the gospel. We had good results in all the schools, but one school in Edmonton, Alberta, was in a league of its own.

When I arrived I discovered that the whole Christian club had been fasting and praying for several days in anticipation of the meeting. The local Teen Challenge director, a Pentecostal minister, had been teaching prayer principles to the students. As soon as I arrived on campus I sensed the presence of the Holy Spirit.

That day the largest room on campus was packed out, and God empowered me to preach as never before. At one point a heckler challenged me and mocked the gospel, but God filled my mind with the details of his life. I shouted out a list of his hidden sins until he left the room.

At the end of the message the students didn't want to leave. The room was filled with small groups of students in earnest conversation, many clustered around the Christians, asking questions about Jesus. It was time to go back to class, but the students ignored the clock. Finally the principal had to ring the fire alarm, vacate the building, line up the students in the snow and march them to their classes.

I felt like Paul at Ephesus during the riot of the god-makers. Seeing such results was wonderful. The truth is, however, that this breakthrough had little to do with my preaching. The hard soil had been ploughed up by those fasting, praying students.

The greatest prayer effort I have witnessed was in Los Angeles during 1983 and 1984. The Olympic outreach is the central illustration of this book, and the prayer strategy and its results are among the most exciting stories of all.

We knew that the attention of the world would be on our city. We expected that hundreds of thousands of foreign visitors would be walking on our streets. This would be a once-in-a-lifetime opportunity for the American church. People from almost every nation on earth would be coming to a city with complete religious freedom, a city already containing resident Christians from at least one hundred different cultures and language groups.

Eventually over sixteen hundred churches united in an active coalition. Ten different subcommittees, dedicated to every conceivable form of evangelism, led us, but we all came together to pray.

Representatives from more than thirty organisations met in a prayer meeting at the Bonaventure Hotel and conceived the outreach. Following that, more than two hundred pastors and Christian leaders met for three days and evenings of prayer at the Salvation Army auditorium on Hollywood Boulevard. Prayer networks were activated across the nation and around the world.

One group of praying women purchased detailed city maps. They spent months praying over the inhabitants of every street. Congregations prayed. Congregations from many churches prayed together at city-wide concerts of prayer. There was even a season of prayer for Los Angeles at an international prayer conference in Korea with more than three hundred thousand intercessors present. Television, magazines and newspapers contained interviews and articles calling for prayer for a great harvest. Most important of all, the pastors of the city began to meet each month for prayer at the Olympic village site.

When the outreach finally began, the spiritual atmosphere of the city had totally changed. Harvest time had come. Teams reported more than a thousand people each day coming to Jesus. I remember teaching on evangelism to six hundred new workers gathered in a Long Beach church. "Satan's power over the city is broken," I said. "Because of all the prayer, the Holy Spirit is working in people's lives right now."

During the break between two teaching sessions I went out and made a phone call at a nearby restaurant. In that twenty minutes, through a set of remarkable circumstances, I managed to lead an engineer from Hughes Aircraft to Christ. "I needed to meet somebody today who knew God," he said, as we tearfully parted. I went back to the class with a story to build their faith for similar divine appointments. In the days that followed everybody led someone to Christ.

During the summer of 1984 the Christians of Los Angeles briefly experienced the reality of a city free from spiritual oppression. The effect on the city was a tantalising illustration of what could be achieved in the years to come as we continue in the battle. Everything in the life of the city was affected. People were friendly and cheerful. Even the summer traffic jams and air pollution failed to materialise. Instead of the expected crime-spree, the crime rate actually dropped.

One of my friends in the police academy chaplaincy programme visited the county morgue shortly after the outreach. A coroner said that normally the morgue received seventy-eight bodies per day, including many who are victims of murder. My friend asked, "Have you ever seen a radical change in these statistics?"

The coroner gave an exciting answer. "Yes," he said, "during the two weeks of the Olympic games there were no murders."

The most lasting legacy of this outreach and perhaps God's true objective was the uniting of scattered, preoccupied spiritual leaders into a coordinated army with a common set of goals. In this unity we found that we had new power to hold back the forces of darkness. We experienced great success in evangelism. We learned to discern the territorial spirits operating over the city and to break their yoke through spiritual warfare.

There are two fundamental steps in spiritual warfare. First, we must discern the nature of the enemy's lie. Then we must exercise the authority of Jesus in order to thwart satanic activity.

The Bible says that Satan is *like* a roaring lion. There is, however, only one lion with true authority and that is the Lion of Judah. Satan's authority becomes a reality only when people succumb to accusation or deception. The Bible says that one day we will look upon the adversary in amazement saying, "Is this the one who shook the earth and the kingdoms of the world?" (Is. 14:16). He will be seen in reality as being small and impotent.

In any conflict for a person, a family, a church or a city, discerning the nature of the enemy's lie is half the battle. Once his deception is exposed, we can see how to apply the specific promises in the Word of God that are the basis of our faith and authority. We see Jesus resisting the devil this way during His time of temptation in the wilderness.

Even if I am interceding for people who embrace and believe the lie of the enemy, such as devout Muslims, I can stand in the gap as a prayer warrior and isolate them from religious spirits or any other form of demonic oppression.

Isaiah 60 says that the people of the earth sit in gross darkness. Can you imagine walking into a darkened room filled with people viewing a multimedia show—people who had never experienced anything other than darkness and the media illusions flickering before them? Imagine walking in, switching on the lights and asking everybody to turn around and observe the mundane equipment responsible for the powerful illusion. That's just how we deal with Satan. He is a projectionist, an illusionist, a deceiver—the father of lies.

Discerning the nature of principalities at work in your city can be as simple as asking God to tell you what's going on. But God also wants us to use our minds in reasoning through the things He has already taught us and in applying them. Genesis 22:17 says, "Your descendants shall possess the gate of their enemies."

In the Bible the city gates represented the place of entrance, authority and decision. We are promised that even the gates of hell will not prevail against the church. In the next section we will examine how to discern the gates of our cities.

Before attempting to rebuild the walls of Jerusalem, Nehemiah carefully surveyed the damage (Neh. 2:13). We, too, must get the big picture before running to the battle. In the next four chapters we will explore essential research in the areas of history, covenants, current revelation and demographics.

SECTION THREE

DISCERNING THE GATES
OF YOUR CITY

*"And I went out by night through the Valley
Gate to the Serpent Well and the Refuse Gate,
and viewed the walls of Jerusalem which were
broken down and its gates which were burned
with fire. "*
Nehemiah 2:13

EIGHT

Looking at History With Discernment

> ". . . You will find in the book of the records and know that this city is a rebellious city, harmful to kings and provinces, and that they have incited sedition within the city in former times, for which cause this city was destroyed. "
>
> Ezra 4:15

Ask yourself the question: why is this city here? Is it merely a product of geography and commerce, or does God have a redemptive purpose in mind for it? Jonah was surprised at the way God looked at Nineveh. Your city is God's city. The people are made in His image. Satan is an invader and a usurper operating in our territory. God did not give demons authority over your city. Demons have infested the earth's atmosphere since before the creation of mankind, but they can only extend their authority into a town or an institution when people sin.

When you look into the history of your city, you will find clues as to what is oppressing the people today. This is our planet, and the only authority Satan has is stolen human authority. He initially gains this authority when, at some point in history, human beings believe his lie, receive his accusation and are seduced into an allegiance to his plan. An obvious example would be the spirit of greed which was let loose during the California gold rush and still dominates the culture of Los Angeles and San Francisco to this day.

Whole countries are kept in darkness by satanic lies that have become cornerstones of a particular culture. Take, for example, the struggle with rejection and the fear of authority experienced by many Australians, because their country originated as a penal colony. Entering through these cruel roots of Australian history, Satan has been able to create a general distrust of all authority figures, including the highest of all who is, of course, God Himself.

The truth is that Australia is not a nation founded on rejection and injustice, but a chosen people with as much dignity and potential as any people in history. They are a people greatly loved by a heavenly Father who is calling them to healing and purpose.

In Sydney in 1979 I witnessed an inter-denominational gathering of fifteen thousand believers making a covenant with God on behalf of their nation. There was spiritual release when one leader led the crowd to extend forgiveness toward Britain for the injustice suffered by their forefathers in the establishment of Australia as a penal settlement.

Prophetic revelation about the purpose and destiny of the nation has been pouring into Australia through its national church ever since. Australian Christians have begun to discover many indicators of God at work even in the earliest days of their national history, and they are filled with faith concerning the future.

Just like those Australian Christians, we need to put today's battles in their historical context. A study of history can give us clues as to God's purpose for a city, and it can also reveal the point at which evil gained entrance. In Ephesians 4:27 we are warned about giving a place of entry to the devil.

Recently while studying the history of a city in California, I came across the specific place and time when Satan seems to have gained entrance. The earliest days in a city's history are very important because one of Satan's main strategies is to interfere with the process of birth. "And the dragon stood before the woman who was ready to give birth, to devour her Child as soon as it was born" (Rev. 12:4).

In this particular town the Christians among the early settlers had gathered together to plan the building of a chapel that would be used alternatively by several compatible congregations, such as Lutherans, Methodists, Presbyterians and Baptists. The process was proceeding smoothly until two prominent citizens had a personality conflict. This outburst of petty bickering eventually led to a rupture of the Christian community into two factions. One hundred years later this town is still marked by division and religious controversy.

What can we do about this today? What can we do now to correct evils that attended our city's birth? Scripture gives us an answer. The Bible exhorts us to prepare the way of the Lord through removing stones of hindrance. "Go through. Go through the gates! Prepare the way for the people; build up, build up the highway! Take out the stones, lift up a banner for the peoples!" (Is. 62:10).

So, through repentance, reconciliation and prayer, the present generation can work to repair the broken–down walls of the city.

> Those from among you
> Shall build the old waste places;
> You shall raise up the foundations of many
>   generations;
> And you shall be called the Repairer of the
>   Breach,

The Restorer of Streets to Dwell In (Is. 58:12).

Restoring unity between our city's churches is an important part of rebuilding the wall. Recently the eldership of an independent charismatic church was in prayer asking God why they could not seem to grow beyond a certain point. The Holy Spirit pointed them toward their roots as a congregation. They did some research and found that their church was birthed when a rebellious faction separated from a downtown Pentecostal church two generations ago.

Even though there was no current animosity between the two churches, the elders went in humility to the mother church and asked for forgiveness in a meeting with the pastor and his board. None of the participants had any memory of these past events, but they sensed that something very important was released through these simple steps of obedience to the Holy Spirit.

When the churches of a city are in unity, they have great power to tear Satan's kingdom up by the roots on a citywide level. In 1988 I had the privilege of ministering among the churches of Reno, Nevada. With an economy built on vice, primarily gambling, Reno is famous for sin.

Fifteen churches came together and rented the dome in the heart of downtown. After I spoke on "Discerning the Gates of Your City," I took the history of the town as a reference point and began to expose the activity of particular spirits. The list included: independence, isolation, self-sufficiency, withdrawal, rebellion, fear of authority, dominance, mammon, love of competition, anger, violence, depression, discouragement, covenant breaking and false comfort.

In many ways Reno is just an exaggeration of the classic Western town that was carved out of the wilderness by fiercely independent people. Today's citizens of Reno still glory in the strength of the individual.

After the message the pastors assembled on the platform and collectively came against the powers of darkness. The first thing they did was to humble themselves. They confessed to having succumbed to the temptations of the city, not the obvious ones like gambling and lust, but the more subtle pressures from independence and isolation.

One brother told the story of his recent confrontation with a motorist. He had almost come to blows with the other driver when he remembered who he was—a pastor representing Christ. "I almost allowed myself to be overcome by the spirit of violence and lawlessness," he said during his prayer of repentance. Many present identified with his confession. As other pastors led the way to the throne of grace, a great cleansing took place that day in the life of the church. Then the pastors abandoned themselves to praise and intercession, which climaxed in a declaration of God's authority over Reno.

The study of a city's history will often reveal the wounds a people have sustained. Some cities carry wounds of rejection or inferiority because they lost their bid to become the state capital, or they were overshadowed by a more successful city nearby. Whole cultures can sustain a wound, which may become a major hindrance to the gospel.

Take Mexico, for example. When dealing with a comparatively new nation like those in the Americas, we must study the experience of the first generation of the native born. Mexicans are a mixture of Spanish and Indian heritage.

Consider the family experience of the first generation of Mexicans. The father was often a white Spaniard, the mother an Indian. Their children were born into a gap between two cultures. A son, for example, wanted to be like his father who is a proud and powerful conquistador, but the centre of warmth and affection was his Indian mother. This foundation experience has greatly hindered the growth of the kingdom of God in Mexico because the image of Father God is distorted.

This understanding directs our strategy in evangelism. Denouncing inappropriate devotion to Mary, which many Mexicans seem to have, will be counterproductive unless we find ways to reveal God the Father in His gentle grace. In the Mexican culture, Jesus is always a baby or a victim. The Father is absent, and Mary is the only approachable paternal figure.

Thousands of statues of the virgin and Child may have more to do with a wounded culture than the doctrines of Catholicism. Before presumptuously praying against religious spirits, we should make sure that we have the true heart and mind of God in the situation.

Exploring history with the Holy Spirit as your guide can be one of the most rewarding preparations for ministry. God may reveal the complex roots of ancient pagan bondage, such as the Roman temple of Mithras, buried under London's streets, or it may be as simple as revelation about the significance of a name.

Have you ever thought about San Francisco? What does that name signify? It speaks of Francis of Assisi, the most radical antimammon prophet of his generation. San Francisco is a trend leader. In a way it's a prophetic city. The city emerged during the greed and immorality of the California gold rush, but God got there first. He marked it with the name of one who prophesied against greed, and He intends to use this city as a trend leader for righteousness. Much work is yet to be done.

Here is a list of key questions to ask when researching your city's history:

1) What place does your city have in this nation's history?
2) Was there ever the imposition of a new culture or language through conquest?
3) What were the religious practices of ancient peoples on the site?
4) Was there a time when a new religion emerged?
5) Under what circumstances did the gospel first enter the city?
6) Has the national or city government ever disintegrated?
7) What has been the leadership style of past governments?
8) Have there ever been wars that affected this city?

   - wars of conquest
   - wars of resistance to invasion
   - civil war

9) Was the city itself the site of a battle?
10) What names have been used to label the city, and what are their meanings?
11) Why was the city originally settled?
12) Did the city have a founder? What was his dream?
13) As political, military and religious leaders have emerged, what did they dream for themselves and for the city?
14) What political, economic and religious institutions have dominated the life of the city?
15) What has been the experience of immigrants to the city?
16) Have there been any traumatic experiences such as economic collapse, race riots or an earthquake?
17) Did the city ever experience the birth of a

socially transforming technology?

18) Has there ever been the sudden opportunity to create wealth such as the discovery of oil or a new irrigation technology?

19) Has there ever been religious conflict among competing religions or among Christians?

20) What is the history of relationships among the races?

You can obtain much information about your city's history through city libraries, museums and historical societies. Perhaps you could begin a filing system for clippings and notes. The prayer life of a church is much more exciting and effective when we make research a habit. You will be surprised at what God reveals to you when you are simply reading the newspaper or browsing in a bookstore.

I recommend becoming prayer and study partners in a movement such as Concerts of Prayer and joining with friends and family in exploring the history of your cities, neighbourhoods, key institutions and historic places.

One local church in Austin, Texas, spent every Saturday afternoon for a year doing prayer walks through every section of the city. This practice is one of the best ways to gain a true understanding of the people God has called us to reach. Pray in every part of the city and allow God to speak to you there. See the whole city as your inheritance.

> For God will save Zion
> And build the cities of Judah,
> That they may dwell there and possess it.
> Also, the descendants of His servants shall
> inherit it,
> And those who love His name shall dwell
> in it (Ps. 69:35-36).

There is one more question I would like to leave with you. You must ask: is there anything in the roots of this city that could be bringing God's judgment rather than His blessing?

For example, we could ask: have we properly dealt with the sin of slavery in the sight of God? While slavery took its course a long time ago in American history, its legacy still haunts the church today. Sunday is the most segregated day of the week. Integration is far more advanced in the worlds of education, commerce and entertainment than in the church. Is there a reason for this?

We have some unfinished business to attend to. One of the reasons for continuing racial prejudice is the unresolved guilt that still resides in the white community. It's time that the curse was lifted and that cleansing and reconciliation came to completion. That's the ministry of Jesus and we are His body.

In one Midwest city that I studied, racially inspired injustice seems to be the only major blot on an otherwise wholesome past. And it all seems to be focused on one shameful incident.

A white mob, outraged over an unsolved crime, lynched an innocent black man. People told me this story as vividly as though it had happened yesterday. Thus, the incident has lost none of its power to create guilt and bitterness, even though it happened many generations ago.

Repentance, reconciliation and healing could take place if Christians from the black and white community joined together in identification with the sins and griefs of their forebears. If the sin is acknowledged and relationship is restored, then the authority of the Lord can be exercised over the demonic forces that have been exploiting the past.

A new resident of the city might think: that's not my problem. I just moved here last year. However, when God puts you in a city you become part of the church there and you inherit its legacy, good or bad. The unfinished business of the church is now your responsibility, too.

I recently discussed this subject with a large gathering of Korean pastors. Because of massive immigration, ten percent of the churches in Los Angeles are now Korean. I talked to my fellow immigrants about the fact that our children and their children after them will be Americans.

Though by birth I am a New Zealander and they are Koreans, we are now part of the American church. We have come to a new battlefield, with new enemies and new allies. We have been summoned to this battle by the Commander-in-chief.

NINE

The History of God's People/Covenants

*"Now therefore, let us make a covenant
with our God...."*   Ezra 10:3

Look into the history of God's people in your city,
particularly at times of revival. God is a covenant–
keeping God, and you may be amazed at the promises
received by past generations as your spiritual forebears
engaged in the same battle.

When we acknowledge and honour those who have
gone before, we are applying the principle of humility.
This process also inspires our faith.

Because of God's covenant with David, Josiah's
generation lived in a time of revival rather than
judgment. If you live in Los Angeles, for example, a
study of the Azusa Street revival might give you insight
into today's battle.

During times of revival, the supernatural realm is

seen with great clarity. Often records are kept and books written that contain important insights. The battle is not new, and we ourselves are the fruit of the powerful labour of past generations. Before we were born, the saints of the past cried out to God for a revelation of Jesus in our generation.

We owe a great debt to people like Wilber Chapman, a Presbyterian evangelist who so stirred the city of Denver to prayer that all business was practically suspended during several busy weekdays in 1905. If you are a Christian in modern Denver, you need to be reminded that in 1921, ten thousand penitents openly sought Jesus as their Saviour during a three-week meeting featuring Aimee Semple McPherson. The whole city was shaken. The mayor and many prominent citizens attended the meetings.

In both cases it was united pastors who supported these evangelists. What did those pastors say to God? More importantly, what did God say to them? Like Josiah of old, we may be surprised to find our names written in a book: "Behold, a child, Josiah by name, shall be born to the house of David" (1 Kin. 13:2). Imagine Josiah's shock when the book of the Law was found during the restoration of the temple and he discovered his own destiny.

Josiah also discovered that his people were under judgment because they had not kept their covenant with God.

> Now it happened, when the king heard the words of the Law, that he tore his clothes....
>
> For great is the wrath of the Lord that is poured out on us, because our fathers have not kept the word of the Lord, to do according to all that is written in this book (2 Chr. 34:19,21).

In many ways this generation is like Josiah's. We are living in a time of certain, but postponed, judgment. Judgment has already been declared and is inevitable but we can turn to God in humility and He will revive us and our children with us.

> "Because your heart was tender, and you humbled yourself before God when you heard His words against this place and against its inhabitants, and you humbled yourself before Me, and you tore your clothes and wept before Me, I also have heard you," says the Lord (2 Chr. 34:27).

It is a dangerous thing to lose the knowledge of the past. "When all that generation had been gathered to their fathers, another generation arose after them who did not know the Lord nor the work which He had done for Israel" (Judg. 2: 10).

One of the greatest needs of the church of the 1990s is a sense of her history and destiny. Have you ever wondered why some cities have repeatedly experienced revival while others have not? Revival by definition is the return of life to that which has died. It means to resuscitate that which was once alive.

The church in many cities has experienced periods of apparent death. What kept it from dying out completely was God, who kept His covenants. In the past, whole generations have lost the knowledge of God, but God kept His promise to their forebears. He sovereignly renewed His kingdom again when He found willing hearts.

God kept His covenant with David during the disintegration of Israel, even though his foolish grandson did not deserve the throne. "But he shall have one tribe for the sake of My servant David, and for the sake of Jerusalem, the city which I have chosen out of all the tribes of Israel" (1 Kin. 11: 32). Note that God had a covenant with the city of Jerusalem as well as with David.

In this regard we need to acknowledge humbly that the Jesus movement of the 1970s was an outpouring of God's mercy on one of the most unworthy generations that has ever existed. We owe a great debt to the saints of the past who founded America in righteousness when they made a covenant on the deck of a little ship named the *Mayflower*.

> But the Lord was gracious to them, had compassion on them, and regarded them, because of His covenant with Abraham, Isaac, and Jacob, and would not yet destroy them or cast them from His presence (2 Kin. 13:23).

When I visited England in 1971, I was impressed by the dark paganism of the place. Cities like London and Bristol contained architectural reminders of past revivals, but I could find only embers of once great fires of the Spirit. In the years since then I have witnessed a steady rekindling of the flame. God is again visiting Britain to the point where I long for such things in America.

No wonder that God has compassion on that land. The vacant-eyed punkers and young urban professionals of British cities are the great-grandchildren of Livingstone, Wesley, Whitefield, Booth, Wycliffe, Fox, Studd and Taylor. The lives of these great heroes of the faith were intercessory acts. Their prayers still ascend before the throne of God. When God weighs Britain in the balance, the scales are heavy with missionary martyrs who gave their lives in Africa and China.

One of the most moving experiences in my life was standing in the room where David Livingstone was born. His early years were spent in poverty in the textile towns of Scotland during the industrial revolution. As I looked through the relics of his life and read of his struggle for Africa, I thought: surely God will always bless Scotland because of this man. Even as I write these words, I am overtaken with weeping because my own ancestors come from this land. Oh, what a heritage undergirds my life as a missionary.

> But the mercy of the Lord is from
>   everlasting to everlasting
> On those who fear Him,
> And His righteousness to children's
>   children,
> To such as keep His covenant,
> And to those who remember His
>   commandments to do them.
> (Ps. 103:17-18)

There are five areas of essential knowledge in which today's Christian worker must walk.

1) *Know the history of the church in your nation.* It may not be possible to know exhaustively the complex history of the American church but we should possess a basic overview. We should be familiar with such things as the values of the pilgrim fathers, the effect of the great awakenings and the lives of personalities like Jonathan Edwards and Charles Finney. If you are a spiritual leader, it is your responsibility to be a steward of our corporate memory, to teach this generation its heritage.

2) *Know the history of the church in your city.* It is possible to be quite familiar with the work of your particular denomination or movement while being appallingly ignorant of the contribution of other groups that are equally important in the sight of God.

3) *Know the history of ministry to your target sub-culture or ethnic group.* If you are working among children, you need to be aware of the American Sunday

school movement. Or if your concern is for American Indians, you have forefathers like the great intercessor David Brainerd, who, in spite of terminal tuberculosis, prayed down revival in 1745.

4) *Know the history of the type of ministry in which you are involved.* If you are in missions, you are walking on a path pioneered by William Carey, Hudson Taylor and Adoniram Judson. If your ministry is theological training, you stand on the shoulders of Wycliffe, Hus and Calvin.

The father of urban missions is undoubtedly William Booth, 1829-1912. He and his Salvation Army pioneered ministry to almost every category of city dweller. They transformed the life of the cities of their day through compassionate attention to the poor, and they boldly confronted evil institutions until they crumbled.

In London the age of consent was only thirteen, and eighty thousand prostitutes, many as young as ten, were sold in the streets or kept in brothels. Booth and his army confronted this evil with holy ferocity and fought until it was outlawed. They lifted a standard of blood and fire which is still the greatest challenge to the life of any urban missionary.

5) *Know the history of your movement.* Do not despise your roots. Every Israelite had a tribe. There were no independent Jews. Sectarian attitudes are wrong, but denominations are biblical. God sets us in families in His kingdom. If you do not know your inheritance, how can you enter into it? How can you rejoice in it?

"The lines have fallen to me in pleasant places; yes, I have a good inheritance" (Ps. 16:6).

Just like the Old Testament tribes, your movement has a corporate past, present and future. Your part of God's family has a gift, a promise and a territory to take. It is essential for me to understand what God has called Youth With a Mission to do if I am to complete successfully the work God has given me to do personally.

I need to be attentive to the original vision of our founder, Loren Cunningham. It is equally important for me to pass on to my staff the promises that God gave to my wife and me when we pioneered this branch of Youth With a Mission many years ago.

"Set up signposts, make landmarks; set your heart toward the highway, the way in which you went" (Jer. 31:21).

A knowledge of history can put everything in perspective. In 1976 I was wandering around the Roman Colosseum on a hot summer day. I glimpsed an ice cream vendor through the ancient stone pillars and walked toward him. When I arrived at the place I first saw him, he had vanished. I searched through the hot ruins, becoming more irritated by the minute. I wanted ice cream!

All of a sudden I saw myself in the sight of God. "For a thousand years in Your sight are like yesterday when it is past" (Ps. 90:4).

Here I was, a twentieth-century believer, moaning about ice cream in the very place where thousands of first-century believers shed their blood for the gospel, and in God's sight it was only yesterday. I was deeply ashamed.

What are you complaining about? It may be something far more difficult than the absence of ice cream, but in the light of history, it may be just as trivial.

The Old Testament prophets, like Ezra, had a sense of the timeless, a sense of time, and a sense of the times in which they lived. Consider the depth of emotion expressed by God's people when they saw God's promise for their city come to pass. Ask yourself if God's purpose for your city means as much to you.

> But many of the priests and Levites and heads of the fathers' houses, who were old men, who had seen the first temple, wept

> with a loud voice when the foundation of
> this temple was laid before their eyes;
> yet many shouted aloud for joy, so that
> the people could not discern the noise of
> the shout of joy from the noise of the
> weeping of the people, for the people
> shouted with a loud shout, and the sound
> was heard afar off   (Ezra 3:12-13).

Finally, a question that can apply to all five categories: *where are the walls of my city broken down ?*

Your forefathers may have obtained promises from God for the city, but perhaps they have never come to pass, because conditions for complete victory have not been met.

Have there ever been strong ministries in the city that rose to a certain point and then failed? What caused that failure? Is there a pattern of defeat in the life of the church?

I know of one city where a strong church emerged that almost took the city for God. Out of this church flowed a stream of life into the other churches of the city. This fountainhead church was loved and respected by all and was like a great shade tree under which many found shelter.

In order to enter the next stage of its inheritance this church needed to be purified and tested. Sadly, the pastor and people were weighed in the balance and found to be unable to enter in. The pastor fell into adultery, and the flock was scattered into bickering factions.

For many years there was no great work of God in that city, then one day a young man came to town as the new pastor of the little church that had once been great. It was a season of harvest. The Jesus movement was just breaking into the youth culture. The church grew until their congregation numbered in the thousands. Once again it became the lead church of the city. Blessing flowed like a river. Large Christian clubs emerged on local high school campuses. A Bible school was established. Missionaries were sent out to the ends of the earth. The churches of the city walked together in harmony, and Christians were admired by the unchurched.

Then it happened. Thirty years after the first failure, the exact same pattern was repeated. The pastor fell into adultery, and the people indulged themselves in an orgy of bitterness and contention. The gospel was mocked in the newspapers, and most congregations lost members until only a remnant was left in the city.

Last year a young man came to town. He came to pastor the church that had once been great. His eyes shine with hope as he looks over the prosperous new suburbs. The town has now grown to a population of a hundred thousand. The future looks bright because the huge metroplex to the south is expanding toward it. Does he know that the walls have been broken down?

O God, help that young man!

TEN

Prophets, Intercessors and Spiritual Fathers

"For by wise counsel you will wage your own war, and in a multitude of counselors there is safety. "

Proverbs 24:6

We have looked at the past to understand the inroads of the enemy, the progress of the battle and the promises of God for our city. Now let's see how to receive the wisdom God has deposited in the saints of today. Has God already given revelation about a strategy for our cities? Is there already a team I should join?

In every city there is a hidden eldership. You will not find this grouping of saints listed in any human book. This circle of mature believers stands in the gap until victory comes.

As Isaiah 62:6-7 says,

> Upon your walls, O Jerusalem, I have set
>   watchmen;
> all the day and all the night they shall
>   never be silent.
> You who put the Lord in remembrance
>   take no rest,
> and give Him no rest
>   until He establishes Jerusalem
>   and makes it a praise in the earth (RSV).

Some of these watchmen are obvious, such as veteran pastors. Others may be obscure intercessors or prophetic people with a hunch. You are on to something if you find a common theme among those who claim revelation.

God always confirms a strategy through several witnesses. This is particularly important when you are dealing with demonic forces. When the spiritual leaders of a city are walking in friendship and respect, then the full power of God can be released against principalities and powers.

An individual ministry or church can achieve a cone of victory within its sphere of service, but the prevailing evil spirits will dominate the secular culture unhindered until the principle of agreement based on harmony in relationships is employed.

Jesus said, "If a kingdom is divided against itself, that kingdom cannot stand" (Mark 3:24). Does this mean that in order to have spiritual power we must all fuse together into one big organisation? Does it mean that we need some kind of citywide eldership, people who sit "in the gate" like the leaders of ancient Hebrew cities?

The issue of ecclesiology is crucial for the nineties, because the changing nature of the city has brought us to a crisis never faced by the church before. The crisis has emerged from the impact of a society of commuters on the life of the local church. For almost two thousand years, a pastor's responsibility has been defined by his parish. The local parish was nearly always seen as the neighbourhoods surrounding the church building.

In the countryside of Holland, people could look up and see the spire of the reformed church nearby. The architecture of the cathedral dominated the skyline of the cities of Christendom for hundreds of years. People literally lived under the shadow of the steeples that called them to worship by the tolling of bells.

If you were an Anglican vicar in England or a Lutheran minister in Germany, you had a sense of territorial responsibility for the people living around the church building. Even in the United States with its history of religious dissent and its overlapping denominational jurisdictions, the pastor could still claim the allegiance of all the Baptists or Presbyterians in a New England village, while he sought to convert the unchurched.

The pastors and priests of the past knew that one day they would have to stand at the judgment seat of Christ and give account for the people of the village, town or neighbourhood near the church. Did everybody have a chance to hear the gospel? Were the children educated? Was there social justice? Were the sick comforted, the believers taught?

Today these simply defined objectives are much less helpful. The city has changed radically. The way people live is now totally different. The contemporary pastor has lost his geographically defined parish. He's not quite sure what his responsibilities are.

People get into their cars on Sunday morning and drive past many other churches on the way to the church of their choice. They even drive past churches whose doctrine they agree with. They choose a church based on a bewildering number of cultural tastes and felt needs. If the church has a programme for teenage children, it will attract some families, while others are looking for rousing worship or deeper teaching. One pastor's congregation lives in every other pastor's backyard. That can be a very threatening situation in an event-oriented culture.

The church has become an institution appealing to the modern commuter within the urban marketplace. Let's look at that marketplace.

In a city like Los Angeles, the average business has access to around two million consumers. In other words, approximately two million people live within a twenty-minute drive of the front door of your place of business. It is so convenient and comfortable in an air-conditioned car that people will cruise down the freeway and think nothing of traversing ten miles of city in order to eat at a particular restaurant or obtain lower prices at a particular store.

What does this mean for the church? The experience of retailers is instructive for the Christian community. In the world of retailing it has meant the emergence of two extremes. On the one hand, specialisation; on the other hand, generalisation.

First of all, specialisation. I know of one retail business in Los Angeles that sells nothing but tennis-shoe laces. That's right, just the laces! You can see the trend even in smaller cities where particular stores specialise in sports shoes, while others sell fashion shoes or children's only or boots.

At the other end of the spectrum is the modern mall. This is a place where you can buy everything under the sun. Growing out of the department store of the forties and the shopping centre of the sixties, the shopping centre has become a city within the city, the return of the village market on a human scale, a town square, a socially important place.

Unconsciously, local churches have adapted to these modern realities. The superchurch is like the modern shopping centre. With its five thousand members, its multifaceted departments and its huge physical plant, it seems as though the whole kingdom of God has come down in one place. These cities of God attempt to meet every conceivable need, drawing people from many miles away.

On the other hand, smaller churches specialise in their ministries, because they cannot compete with the resource–rich superchurch.

Is this a positive development? That depends on our response to the temptations and possibilities presented to us by this new environment. We have never faced a greater temptation to divide one from another. In an open market of free-wheeling consumers, a pastor competes not only with other pastors, but all kinds of other ministries influence his people, creating lines of allegiance and financial support. Radio "ministers" such as James Dobson talk to a pastor's congregation as they drive to work. Bible teachers such as Bill Gothard draw thousands from across the city. Evangelists lead our people in outreach to the streets.

The adage "Tithe where you're fed," if actually acted upon, will not put 10 percent in the hands of the local church. The Bible says to bring the whole tithe into the storehouse, but people are becoming more and more ambivalent about what the word *storehouse* defines.

Never before in history have spiritual leaders faced such a temptation to tighten their control of people and divide from one another. In the future there may be an attack on the doctrine of other churches, but in most cases the real issue will be power and money.

After all, because of the very factors I have mentioned, the doctrine of the church is becoming more and more uniform (and orthodox at that). We live so close together with such good communications, that it has become increasingly difficult to hold heretical views and get away with it. If we preach a strange gospel, our people will soon tell us about it; they have immediate access to hundreds of other preachers through Christian books, magazines, radio and TV.

What is the answer? To put it bluntly, "If you can't

beat'em, join 'em." This could be the greatest season of unity since the days of the early church, when the church was simply called "the church of Ephesus" (Rev. 2:1) or "the church of God which is at Corinth" (1 Cor. 1:2).

What a blessing it must have been to sense the camaraderie of the early church in Jerusalem. "Now the multitude of those who believed were of one heart and one soul" (Acts 4:32). Will we ever see such unity again? In spirit, yes. In structure, no.

The early church in Jerusalem cannot be compared to the church in a modern world-class city because the scale is totally different. The best biblical comparison is with Israel as a nation. Many supercities of today are much larger than the entire population of ancient Israel. The question then becomes, how did God govern Israel?

Israel was divided into tribes. Above the level of the tribe, God Himself reserved the right to govern. The prophet Samuel warned that Israel's experiment with a monarchy would be a negative experience. This proved to be true and quickly led to national division and captivity.

God's highest form of government for Israel involved these three factors:

1) *Law and covenants.* His promise to Abraham; the Ten Commandments, and so on.
2) *The presence of His Spirit*, which included His re–lationship with each person; the cloud in the wil–derness; His presence in the tabernacle and so on.
3) *The role of judges.* Prophets like Samuel and task leaders like Gideon, who emerged by God's own appointment.

In a particular tribal territory the people had an eldership, as did a town or even a village, if it had at least 120 residents. Land was held by family groupings. Leadership was appointed in areas of military, judicial and civic life. However, on a national level, Israel had

only one true king: God Himself.
   This is also God's purpose for the church.

> For unto us a Child is born.
> Unto us a Son is given;
> And the government will be upon His
>   shoulder.
> And His name will be called
> Wonderful, Counselor, Mighty God,
> Everlasting Father, Prince of Peace.
> Of the increase of His government and
>   peace
> There will be no end (Is. 9:6-7).

The word of the Lord to the church of the 1990s is this: *the government shall rest on the shoulders of Jesus.*

We must avoid at all costs a structure that is marked by the enemy. Satan would scatter us to the four winds or join us into a false unity that stifles the freedom of the church in all its diversity.

God's kingdom is a kingdom of liberty in which everything is permitted unless specifically prohibited. Satan's kingdom is a controlled hierarchy in which nothing is permitted unless authorised. God, because of His omnipresence, can safely decentralise without losing control; Satan fears the loss of control and draws everything into a pyramid of power with himself at the centre.

God often unites a city around a dynamic vision such as a Billy Graham crusade, but I have yet to see the leadership of one of these coalitions form into a permanent eldership with God's blessing upon it.

Through the years I have served an apprenticeship under many wise leaders who have called the city to unity. In 1980 I was on the board of a coalition that drew thirty-seven thousand people to a stadium to celebrate Christian unity and raise funds for organisations working with Cambodian refugees. In

1981 I was on the board of another coalition that drew fifty thousand Christians to the Rose Bowl. In 1982 it was a combined evangelistic outreach and Jesus festival. In 1983 we began preparations for the Olympic Games Outreach.

It seems that each year God anoints new leadership with a fresh vision. Each year the circle of loving friendship becomes larger, but we have to pass a collective test of humility as we recognise and then follow the new leadership that God Himself has appointed. It's as though God draws a line in the dust saying, "Who is on the Lord's side? Cross over to Me here."

The hand of the Lord once came upon a man named Gideon, and God used him to win a great victory. Upon his return from the battle, the people crowded around him saying,

> "Rule over us, both you and your son, and your grandson also; for you have delivered us from the hand of Midian." But Gideon said to them, "I will not rule over you, nor shall my son rule over you; the Lord shall rule over you." (Judg. 8:22-23)

This was the Scripture that God gave me in 1984. We had enjoyed such success in the Olympic outreach that I came under great pressure from other leaders to come up with another unifying vision. The Lord used the story of Gideon to warn me. In effect, God told me to go back to my own organisation and take care of my normal responsibilities. The fact that He had used me once to gain a victory was a manifestation of His sovereignty and grace, not evidence of any qualifying ability of mine.

We must have faith in God's ability to anoint and appoint new leadership with fresh vision. We must have humility as we step aside from temporary responsibilities and recognise the new leadership that God is raising up.

If we are not to have a permanent citywide structure, then what are we to have? Much understanding can be gained by studying the concept of eldership as it is exemplified in the New Testament.

Because of bold preaching, the island of Crete was filled with new converts, and Paul delegated to young Titus the responsibility of organising them. "For this reason I left you in Crete, that you should set in order the things that are lacking, and appoint elders in every city as I commanded you" (Titus 1:5).

Much could be said about the need for plurality of leadership and the function of eldership in local churches, but I want to focus on just one implication of Paul's strategy. The apostle Paul was more concerned with spiritual authority than with tidy organisational models. He knew that the kingdom of God is truly established when a circle of believers is joined together in covenantal love. He also knew that the new churches would come under satanic attack.

The New Testament uses two different Greek words to describe elders: *presbuteros* and *episkopos*. These words indicate a circle of wise, experienced Christians guarding and covering the flock of God. Take special note of the idea imparted by the word *episkopos*, which has a root meaning "to watch over" or "to cover".

Most readers of this book will be seated indoors. If that applies to you, look up at the roof above your head. Why is it there? It's not holding the walls up; it's not keeping the people in; it has been built primarily to keep something out. The roof protects you from the wind and the rain.

When Paul directed that the believers be covered by an eldership, he was trying to protect them from accusation and deception, which are the main devices that Satan uses against people. A prime responsibility of an elder is to nurture affectionate relationships with other elders, so that no gap is left for the entrance of the enemy.

God still uses this principle today. Right now God is at work within your city, increasing the circle of covenantal love. God organises His kingdom through gifts of friendship. The body of Christ in an American city is too large and complex for any person or group to govern. However, God is weaving relationships into an invisible matrix of ministries that cover the city. Many Christians may live in the city, but the true size of the church in birth potential is proportional to the number of believers walking in relational harmony.

Does this mean that we need to know every last believer in order to gain authority over principalities? Of course not, but it does mean that I need to know and appreciate the ministries and movements within the city. I must be a loyal member of my local church, but I also need to befriend and serve people from other parts of God's kingdom as well.

The family of God is incredibly diverse, yet many sincere believers are ignorant of the importance of having many ministries. Once I was talking to a Christian leader in a youth ministry, when he said to me, "If the local church was doing its job, we wouldn't need to have special ministries like this."

I didn't know whether to laugh or cry. What an incredible pressure we put on local churches to be the whole kingdom of God represented in one place. No wonder pastors feel such stress. They feel obligated to meet everybody's expectations. The result is disappointment and discouragement.

There is no absolute model for what a local church should be. I once spent an afternoon with over one hundred spiritual leaders from several denominations. We tried to come up with a universal definition of a biblical local church. You may think that it was an easy task, but if you consider all the cultures and circumstances of people on the earth and you examine the diversity of models in the Bible, you will begin to understand our frustration. After many hours of discussion, we had produced many good models, but no absolute definition other than "people moving together under the lordship of Jesus."

To build a mental model of the ideal local church and to impose it upon ourselves is to participate in cultural idolatry. We are not called to build model ministries but to build the kingdom of God in our city.

The great blessing of the kingdom is not sameness and uniformity but creativity and diversity. A local church will never do the job of Wycliffe Bible Translators, and Wycliffe will never do the job of Campus Crusade for Christ. Praise God for that!

We don't need to compete. We must be honest about our weaknesses, contribute with our strengths and celebrate with joy the great diversity of ministries given to our generation by God.

I love the people of God. I love the churches and organisations that I have had the privilege of working with. Their uniqueness makes them valuable. Their basic differences reveal the complete picture of the beauty of Jesus to the city. Others' gifts humble me. I desperately need my brothers and sisters in the other tribes of Israel. I dare not become consumed by a vision of my own little corner of the vineyard. I must have a heart for God's kingdom, not mine.

The prophet Haggai rebuked the people of his day for retreating to their own little territory and forgetting their corporate mandate.

> "You looked for much, but indeed it came to little; and when you brought it home, I blew it away. Why?" says the Lord of hosts. "Because of My house that is in ruins, while every one of you runs to his own house.
> "Therefore the heavens above you

withhold the dew, and the earth withholds
its fruit" (Hag. 1:9-10).

All right, let's get practical. What can we personally
do about all this? We have learned that our
relationships with one another form the invisible walls
of the city and that lack of relationship or broken
relationships can hinder the effectiveness of our
prayers. However, what are the positive actions we can
take to discern Christ's body and build up the wall?

The following is a list of questions that will help you
to discover the ministries that God has placed in your
city. We need to love them, serve them and humbly
receive ministry from them.

1) What is the total number of churches in the
city?
2) Are the churches concentrated in some sections
while absent in others?
3) Which churches are evangelical?
4) Which churches are active and growing?
5) Are there dynamic churches present in every
ethnic group?
6) Look over a list of churches and see if you can
discern a particular gift expressed by each
congregation. What is unique about its
ministry?

Recently I talked to a pastor who was
approached by some of his people about
starting a singles' department. He was feeling
stirred toward another emphasis at that time,
so he recommended that they join the growing
singles' ministry of the Assemblies of God
church a few blocks away. He did not see this
as an admission of failure to produce the
perfect church. He saw his brother pastor as
another member of the leadership team that
God had assembled to take the city.

7) Obtain a list of the Christian organisations in the city. Do you really understand what God has called each one to do?

8) Identify the senior leaders of ministries and churches. What are they saying about the state of the church? Do they have a vision for the future?

9) Who are the emerging leaders? What is their message?

One of the best ways to obtain this information is to contact organisations that already have a citywide vision, including denominational headquarters, missions societies, prayer movements and seminaries or Bible schools with an emphasis on urban missions.

It is also important to recognise that God still sends to cities prophets who hold a plumbline to the structures we are building. "So the elders of the Jews built, and they prospered through the prophesying of Haggai the prophet and Zechariah the son of Iddo" (Ezra 6:14).

It is now a season for the restored prominence of the ministry of apostles and prophets who will lay the foundations for the coming move of God. We have experienced many decades of emphasis on the ministry of evangelists, teachers and pastors, but God is now restoring our understanding of the fivefold ministry for the equipping of the saints (see Eph. 4:11-13).

Prophets feature prominently alongside the ministry of the apostles in the New Testament. While Paul and Barnabas were ministering in Antioch, they were served by other members of the travelling church:

> And in these days prophets came from Jerusalem to Antioch. Then one of them, named Agabus, stood up and showed by the Spirit that there was going to be a great famine throughout all the world,

which also happened in the days of Claudius Caesar (Acts 11 :27-28).

In summary, then, do these four things:

1) Know the church, its movements and the ministries given to people.
2) Listen for the sound of the trumpet. "He who has an ear, let him hear what the Spirit says to the churches" (Rev. 2:7).
3) Receive God-given gifts of friendship and walk in covenant with believers from fellowships other than your own.
4) Join with those who call the church to unity.

While writing this chapter, I had the delightful experience of speaking at a Night of Missions, in Ventura, California. The event was sponsored by several local churches and organised by Youth With a Mission.

The auditorium was crowded with people of all ages who watched a powerful multimedia on the unfinished task of world evangelisation, followed by the presentation of twelve different ministries. It was a night of celebration. We experienced times of deep conviction and times of hilarity as the wonderful diversity of the kingdom unfolded before our eyes.

Here is a sample of some of the ministries: a theatrical ministry, a group that drills wells in Uganda, Wycliffe Bible Translators, an unwed mother's home, a musical ministry to children, a short-term outreach to Mexico, a foreign outreach for Christian surfers and a mission to Eastern Europe.

We went over to the fellowship hall to look at booths and displays with a sense of wonder and joy at being included in such an interesting family– the family of God.

> Behold, how good and how pleasant it is
> For brethren to dwell together in unity!
> (Ps. 133:1)

110

ELEVEN

Get the Facts

"The heart of him who has understanding seeks knowledge."　　　Proverbs 15:14

It is amazing to me how uninformed we are of the basic realities around us. Do you know your city? You should have the census in one hand and the Bible in the other. What percentage of people actually attend church? How many people are in poverty? Why are they in poverty? Where do they live? Are there subcultures, ethnic groups, changes in the economy, an ageing population? What's really going on? You need to know if you are going to help free your city from evil spiritual dominance.

Spiritual warfare does not operate in a vacuum. It is the air force that covers the soul winner and the evangelist, and all evangelism must be carefully conducted using all available information.

First, get out a map of the city. Study it carefully. See if you can identify concentrations of the elderly, the homeless, students, children and so on. Which subcultures are more receptive than others to the gospel? Why? What are the felt needs of the people of the city? Gather evidence to demonstrate your conclusions.

Parts of the city may vary greatly in culture, crime levels and wealth. Try to determine the felt needs of each group of people.

What you research depends on your goals. A pastor planting a church or an evangelist planning an outreach will need very specific information and statistics. However, all of us are called to the ministry of intercession and thus need to have some knowledge of the big picture.

If we are to be more like Jesus, we must have a broad perspective. The Bible says, "Let this mind be in you which was also in Christ Jesus" (Phil. 2:5), which means to have not only the attitudes but also the perspective of Jesus.

God told Moses to get the facts as the initial step that would lead the Jews into their inheritance: "Send men to spy out the land of Canaan, which I am giving to the children of Israel; from each tribe of their fathers you shall send a man, every one a leader among them" (Num. 13:2).

It is important to see research as an exercise for spiritually mature, proven leadership. Moses specifically commissioned the spies to assess the strength of the enemy, a job that is not for the fainthearted. "And see what the land is like: whether the people who dwell in it are strong or weak, few or many; whether the land they dwell in is good or bad; whether the cities they inhabit are like camps or strongholds" (Num.13: 18 -19).

After forty days the spies returned with totally

different assessments, even though they had all been exposed to the same facts. The majority lost sight of God's greatness, saying, "The land through which we have gone as spies is a land that devours its inhabitants, and all the people whom we saw in it are men of great stature" (Num. 13:32).

In today's vast cities we need people of faith, like Joshua and Caleb, who see hope for the future even in the presence of powerful enemies.

> Then Caleb quieted the people before Moses, and said, "Let us go up at once and take possession, for we are well able to overcome it."...
>
> And they spoke to all the congregation of the children of Israel, saying: "The land we passed through to spy out is an exceedingly good land.
>
> "If the Lord delights in us, then He will bring us into this land and give it to us, 'a land which flows with milk and honey'.
>
> "Only do not rebel against the Lord, nor fear the people of the land, for they are our bread; their protection has departed from them, and the Lord is with us. Do not fear them" (Num. 13:30; 14:7-9).

We must have a mature faith when we deal with the complex bureaucracy of state and city agencies. For instance, if you are starting a new ministry, never send an immature believer to inquire of the city about zoning or permits.

I was once involved in pioneering a preschool. We found ourselves relating to nine different governmental agencies. Several times I was told by members of my staff that it was impossible to proceed, because some code or ordinance forbade it. I would go back to God, and He would tell me, "Keep going; trust Me; there is a way."

Red tape is often the easiest way for the enemy to defeat the birth or expansion of a local church. Regulatory agencies are not our enemy. They have a valid servant function, but they can be lawfully circumvented. For example, a church can get a conditional use permit for construction of a building in an area zoned by the city for another purpose.

The expense and complexity of dealing with local government is one of the most intimidating aspects of urban ministry. Remember the facts that are repeated to you are not always the truth as God would see it. God has more creative ways to fulfil His word than you could ever imagine.

God can provide the money to bring your buildings up to legal standards. God can make a way through the labyrinth of overlapping jurisdictions. Do not lose heart, for nothing is too difficult for Him. The key is to live by every word that proceeds out of His mouth, even if human voices tell you that it can't be done.

I love the attitude of Joshua and Caleb. They loved Canaan and they were not afraid. I often have to listen to Christian workers confessing that they really hate big-city urban life, and that if they stay, it will be a big sacrifice.

God showed me the root of this attitude. Satan mainly attacks the urban Christian through fear. We have a hard time loving the city, because we are afraid that living there may hurt us or our loved ones. But by the power of the Holy Spirit, we can replace fear with love. The Bible says, "Perfect love casts out fear" (1 John 4:18).

As you study crime statistics; as you contemplate the enormous expense of renting a facility in the city; as you look at abuse and abortion trends, make sure you don't take your eyes off the living God, who reigns from His throne.

Ask God to fill you with His divine perspective. Those statistics are actually people known intimately by

Him. Let His Spirit move upon your spirit. Let Him break your heart and fill you with compassion. Let Him lift up your head and fill your mouth with praise. Let Him fill your mind with His intention for the city.

You may not think of yourself as a prophet, but, like Daniel of old, you can call upon the God who "reveals deep and secret things; He knows what is in the darkness, and light dwells with Him" (Dan. 2:22).

In the modern city the only constant is change. The statistics we are able to gather are often outdated, so we must be future-oriented. Trends and their implications must be examined to plan new ministries and churches or renew old ones.

The Youth With a Mission staff stationed in Los Angeles recently met together for a strategy day. The teams came in from all over the city with research materials that they had gathered, and we worked on our plans for the future. We reduced our pile of statistics and news clippings to a small list of trends affecting our metro area. It soon became obvious to all that a new vision for ministry to children and ethnic groups was imperative. I have included our trends list as an example.

Toward 2000: Eighteen Trends in LA

1) A continuing increase in population through high birth rates and immigration.

   California (1989)....27 million
   California (2020).....40 million

2) The continuing influx of large waves of immigrants from foreign countries further expanding the common culture of diversity with no predominant culture.

3) An increase in wealth and influence for cities in the metropolitan Los Angeles area.

In 1989 the metroplex has 157 separate incorporated cities, ranging in size from Los Angeles (3.3 million residents) to Vernon (ninety residents). It is first among U.S. cities in manufacturing shipments valued at $75.7 billion in 1986 compared with $71.5 billion for second-ranked Chicago. Los Angeles is a major tourist destination with seventy-seven million visitors a year, and one of the primary attractions is shopping. It is the headquarters for the U.S. subsidiaries of eleven foreign auto firms. It houses the offices of 120 foreign banks and would rank tenth among the nations of the world in terms of gross product.

The Los Angeles area's estimated 1986 product of $275 billion would put it ahead of Brazil, India, Mexico, Australia, Spain, The Netherlands and Switzerland. California has the seventh largest economy in the world.

4) The emergence of the Pacific Rim marketplace as the dominant theatre of world trade.

Los Angeles serves this market as the primary port of entry to the American market and prime location for Pacific Basin businesses such as corporate headquarters and financial services.

5) The Asianisation of Los Angeles in culture, politics and economics.

In 1985 the Asian population was 792,000. And while Asian Americans will probably never be the most numerous ethnic group, they are already affecting the city far out of proportion to their numbers. Between now and 2010, the Asian population is expected to swell by one million people, raising its share of the area's total population to nearly 10 percent.

6) The gentrification or Manhattanisation of the city centres, displacing the indigent and welfare-dependent families from their traditional environment in the inner city. The development of new pockets of poverty in blighted, suburban neighbourhoods and parks.

7) The polarisation of the population into rich and poor in the urban landscape due to a rapid rise in urban land values. The emergence of a per–manent underclass of renting urban dwellers.

8) The city will move up, not out, as remaining open land is developed and redevelopment zones replace substandard housing with new upscale architecture.

   Federal tax law is slanted in a way that leads ultimately to demolition of blighted neighbourhoods, yet no alternative low-rent housing is available for poor families. There will be a trend toward multiple families living in suburban tract houses and apartments. Homelessness will increase, including families from other states and many people who are fully employed.

9) The development of built-up, mass transit corridors surrounding light rail and under–ground transportation surface stations.

   This will lead to the development of several foot-traffic entertainment and retail centres, which will provide population access for evangelism.

10) Even if other parts of the nation experience recession, personal, disposable income will steadily increase for working people, who will spend it on education, recreation and travel.

   Continuing education for adults and private education for children will increase significantly. Demand will grow for preschools, day care and related services for children.

11) An ageing population, with the majority of its members between the ages of twenty and forty-four.

   The youngest population will be found in suburbs with a high percentage of immigrants. Some school districts will close schools, while others will continue to be severely over-crowded.

12) Continuing family disintegration.

   Even though the divorce rate is stabilising, the experience of children is still moving away from a two-parent family. Only a tiny minority of children comes home to a mother who is a homemaker, even if the parents are still together.

13) Continuing crisis in public education.

   Largely due to the deterioration of com-munity and family life, gangs, criminal be-haviour among children, teenage pregnancy and drug addiction will be typical. A desperate school system could become open to Christian ministries in certain forms as they did during the early seventies during a drug epidemic. For example, the environment will be open to such ministries as Choose Life seminars, designed to combat suicide. (At thirty-eight thousand per year, suicides in California are 16 percent above the national average.)

14) AIDS will continue to spread rapidly into the heterosexual community.

   However, in spite of fear, the tendency toward sexual promiscuity will be slow to change, particularly in black, white and Hispanic teens. This will lead to an increase in teen suicide.

15) The national self-concept is gradually changing from the Puritan-generated dream of a nation of servant ideals (for example, refuge and

outreach) to a nation dominated by conquest ideals (for example, fame, wealth and power).

We now as a people value unbridled liberty in the cause of personal success more than service. At present the secular culture is pre–dominantly turning away from idealism, such as we saw in the sixties, and turning toward the pursuit of affluence, security and status. Even middle-class children are money-minded and career–conscious. Southern California is a primary contributor to this dream of a hedonistic life-style.

16) In Christianity, the trend is toward strong ethnic movements particularly among Koreans and Hispanics.

17) Los Angeles will continue to be a trend-setting city due to expanding media, political and economic power.

The life-style of the city will come under increasing scrutiny as the population climbs rapidly toward first place among U.S. cities.

18) A chain of large cities is developing along the U.S.-Mexican border due to offshore manufacturing policies.

These cities such as El Paso-Juarez and San Diego-Tijuana are becoming magnets for millions of economic refugees from the south. The U.S.-Mexican border represents the greatest contrast between wealth and poverty in the world, presenting an enormous challenge both to governments and to Christian agencies. The Los Angeles job market is the main target of illegals crossing the border.

This may seem like a complex body of information. However, you and your associates can gather similar data on your town. Ask yourself: what do you see happening in your city in the next twelve years?

In projecting the future of your city, you will find that some trends are common knowledge, while others will be discovered only through statistical analysis and careful calculation. Statistical information can be gleaned from the state almanac, the census and United Way publications and by clipping and filing articles from the daily newspapers.

When you have projected your own list of trends, ask yourself the following questions:

1) Which trends represent the greatest opportunity for the entrance of the gospel? (For example, an influx of refugees.)
2) Is there an approaching crisis that should become the focus of intense prayer and ministry? (For example, an increase of homelessness or unemployment.)
3) Will existing Christian organisations and churches be hurt by demographic changes such as ethnicity, age and economics?
4) Where will the church continue to grow? (For example, among Hispanics and in new middle-class housing tracts.)
5) Is there a particular subculture that is manifesting an unusual level of satanic oppression? (For example, a sudden upsurge in teen suicide.)
6) Which subculture is experiencing the greatest degree of spiritual darkness?
7) Which subculture represents the poorest of the poor, the most vulnerable and needy group in the city?
8) What are the opportunities for partnership between spiritually dynamic churches and struggling congregations and ministries in other neighbourhoods?
9) Are there sociological groups that are actually calling for help?(For example, gang-infested

neighbourhoods or single mothers.)

10) What is the social issue stirring the greatest community concern in each section of the city? (For example, AIDS, racial tension or property taxes.)

11) What do these trends reveal about the nature of the unseen realm over the city?

12) Is the ministry of your church or organisation properly targeted?

When we have a working knowledge of the city, we are able to receive revelation from God about a specific strategy for ongoing evangelism and discipleship. In the next section we will cross over Jordan and begin to fight.

SECTION FOUR

LEARNING TO FIGHT

Foundational truths of spiritual warfare

"The serpent you shall trample underfoot. "
Psalm 91:13

TWELVE

Born to Battle

*"So the great dragon was cast out, that
serpent of old, called the Devil and
Satan,who deceives the whole world; he
was cast to the earth, and his angels were
cast out with him. "*   Revelation 12:9

Once we have discerned the gates of our city—
assessed its spiritual condition—we are ready to act.
The purpose of this section is to help us to understand
more fully the realities of the spiritual realm. We
prepare for spiritual warfare by understanding our
provision as believers for exercising the Lord's
authority over His enemies. We will then be ready to
come against our city's spiritual strongholds more
effectively.

Human history is a story of perpetual struggle
against the emissaries of evil. The question is: what are
all these demons doing here anyway? How did we get
to be on a planet so infested with evil?

The Bible teaches that angels were created to be holy

(Gen.1:31), but at some point before the creation of man, a portion of the angels entered into deliberate rebellion against God. These rebellious angels were judged by God. Some were chained in hell (2 Pet. 2:4), but others were left free to oppose God and His kingdom.

Why would God do that? Why would He leave a free force in opposition to Himself? I believe it is because the development of man in his ultimate potential depended on an experience with an adversary. That's right, God wanted us to learn to fight.

Man a warrior race, made in God's own image and destined to rule beside Him. Intrinsic to our nature is the drive to conquer something, to control something. This desire can be perverted in lusting after power for pride's sake or converted and harnessed in the benevolent government of God's own kingdom. We are destined to rule with Christ.

Fashioned from the redeemed children of Adam, a bride is emerging that will enter into the fellowship of the triune God at the marriage supper of the Lamb (Rev. 19:5-9). But before eternity comes a brief experience of earthbound battle. Think of God's original directive to man and woman in Genesis 1:28: "Be fruitful and multiply; fill the earth and subdue it; have dominion over the fish of the sea, over the birds of the air, and over every living thing that moves on the earth." Note the word *subdue*, implying an adversarial position. God did not use a word like *cultivate*. He knew that a person would enter his or her inheritance only by taking dominion.

God's ultimate motive was to create mankind for a loving relationship with Himself. There are three essential aspects to any relationship: shared presence, exploration of traits and character, and mutual responsibility. It is in preparation for the third category that we find the reason for this terrestrial apprenticeship.

God is planning to share with us not only the

intimacy of relationship but also the responsibility of governing the universe in justice and mercy. We are to govern in agape love, self-sacrificing love.

God has marked out for us a personal inheritance. Our success will not be demonstrated by the fact that we lie down in death and are able to say, "I'm still saved and my children and grandchildren are all in the kingdom." That's only part of it.

As we press in to know God, He unfolds to us revelation about a personal destiny. We have places to go and people to bless. We have been given a gift, a promise and a territory to take.

As we communicate the gospel, raise children, and cultivate the earth's resources, we will face the harassment of demons. They have been left here by God just for us to practise on. These demons have already been defeated and judged, but our privilege is "to execute on them the written judgment" (Ps. 149:9).

I believe our experience parallels the experience of Joseph in the Bible. He suffered terribly through his apprenticeship for leadership because his jealous brothers sold him into slavery. Many years later these same brothers came before Joseph, the ruler, and heard him say, "You meant evil against me; but God meant it for good" (Gen. 50:20).

A time is coming when we, the bride of Christ, will be able to say to the host of fallen angels, "You attempted to enslave us on a dark and fallen planet. You meant it for evil but our God has used the experience to prepare us to rule."

This brings us the answer to the question: why does God allow evil to be present in the earth? Of course, the potential for evil is present within humankind's state of moral freedom, our freedom to choose. However, that does not address the issue of demons.

Lucifer and the rebellious angels were present on this planet at the time of the creation of the human race. Since the fall of Adam and Eve, diabolical influence has become pervasive in human cultures because of continuing sin.

We who follow Jesus now face a task similar to the children of Israel after crossing the Jordan into the promised land. They entered into the land by faith, just as we enter into salvation by faith. Then they faced the task of defeating the Canaanites.

In Judges 3:1-2, there is reference to the Canaanite tribes left in the land after the death of Joshua, followed by this interesting statement: "This was only so that the generations of the children of Israel might be taught to know war, at least those who had not formerly known it."

Does God still want us to know war? Is it still part of His plan to develop us as warriors? Yes. We are to partner with God in the battle. The New Testament believer is applying the resurrection power of Jesus. "For the weapons of our warfare are not carnal but mighty in God for pulling down strongholds" (2 Cor. 10:4).

This hostile environment is essential for our eternal future. Mankind has been made to take dominion. It is necessary that we face an antagonist during our brief apprenticeship on earth to qualify in character to rule with Christ in eternity.

All About Evil Spirits

Before going on to explore the tactics of our warfare we must become familiar with what the Bible reveals about Satan's kingdom. Here is a brief summary including Scripture references for your further study.

Begin by meditating on these two important passages:

> He has delivered us from the power of darkness and translated us into the kingdom of the Son of His love (Col. 1:13).

...having wiped out the handwriting of requirements that was against us, which was contrary to us. And He has taken it out of the way, having nailed it to the cross.

Having disarmed principalities and powers, He made a public spectacle of them, triumphing over them in it.
(Col. 2:14 - 15)

1) Assuming that Isaiah 14:12-15 refers to the devil (as church tradition has taught), he is called "Shining One" in that passage. From the Latin translation of that title we get the name Lucifer.
2) God divided responsibility among several high-ranking angels. One of these angels was named Lucifer. He may have been an archangel, although Michael is the only one specifically called an archangel in the Bible (Jude 1:9).
3) Through rebellion, Lucifer fell from heaven taking one third of the angels with Him. Every free moral creature in the universe must at one time make a final decision whether to give allegiance to God or to self. Lucifer chose self. (Rev. 12:7-9)
4) Some of the fallen angels were cast down to hell and chained until judgment day while others were left free to oppose God and His kingdom (2 Pet. 2:4).
5) Lucifer became the adversary, which is the meaning of the name Satan. He is the enemy of both God and man. Satan is filled with vindictive rage against the redeemed children of Adam, who will rule with Christ in glory.
6) Satan and his fallen angels were defeated at the cross and will finally be condemned (Col. 2:15; Matt. 25:41).
7) Demons are the force operating behind false religions, idolatry, magic and witchcraft

(Deut. 32:17; Ps. 96:5;1 Cor. 10:19-20; Rev. 9:20-21).

8) Satan and demons are in a state of continual war against the church, and all believers are exhorted to combat all levels of evil spiritual force in the unseen realm (Eph. 6:10-15).

9) Demons are permitted by God to tempt and deceive in a limited way, but they cannot override the human will (1 Cor. 10:13; Job 1:12).

10) Demons are allowed limited control over natural phenomena within the earth's atmosphere (Job 1:19).

11) Satan has two primary characteristics, which are also his weapons against humanity and the church: he is an accuser and a deceiver (Rev. 12:7-10).

12) The Bible records characteristics of demonic oppression such as mental anguish, physical sickness, masochism, nakedness and the inability to speak (Matt. 8:28-33; Mark 5:1-6; Luke 8:26-39; Matt. 9:32).

13) Satan has assigned certain demons to certain territories, nations, cities and subcultures. These demons seek to pervert the people in their territory and to turn them against God.

   For example, Ezekiel 28:12 contains ref–erence to the king of Tyre. In the context of the passage, it seems that the Spirit of God is not referring to an earthly ruler but to a prin–cipality or power, such as those referred to in Ephesians 6:12.

14) Jesus demonstrated His power over demons and has passed this power on to His followers (Mark 16:17; Rev. 12: 11).

Far more important than the study of angels and demons is the study of God Himself. Consider this passage from the book of Revelation 19:4-6:

And the twenty-four elders and the four living creatures fell down and worshiped God who sat on the throne, saying, "Amen! Alleluia!"

Then a voice came from the throne, saying, "Praise our God, all you His servants and those who fear Him, both small and great!"

And I heard, as it were, the voice of a great multitude, as the sound of many waters and as the sound of mighty thunderings, saying, "Alleluia! For the Lord God Omnipotent reigns!"

This is the sound of heaven exulting over the destruction of the works of Satan in the final judgment. I can't wait! One thing is certain. To follow Jesus is to march toward a final and complete victory.

THIRTEEN

The Unseen Realm

We do not look at the things which are seen, but at the things which are not seen. For the things which are seen are temporary, but the things which are not seen are eternal." 2 Corinthians 4:18

What is the enemy doing in your city? True to his nature, he's probably setting fires. You can rush around putting out the fires, or you can capture and sentence the arsonist.

When we look at the kingdom of God, we don't focus on the gifts but the Giver. Jesus is the centre of our attention. We should take a similar approach to the kingdom of darkness.

We should not focus on the evil, while ignoring the evil one. We tend to look at problems caused by fallen angels without seeing them as the cause. In the daily newspaper we read reports of gang violence, corrupt government and child abuse, without clearly establishing the connection to the very real conflict in the unseen realm.

Christians are called to operate in the unseen realm. We must take initiative to take territory from Satan. Many believers practise deliverance on a small scale, such as the freeing of individuals, but then see large-scale problems only as consequences of social or political processes.

I am committed to political and social action, but I realise that electing good people to office is not half as important as gaining victory over principalities through united prayer.

The rightly prioritised agenda of a biblical believer should be personal repentance and holy living, leading to united prayer, to revival of the church, to awakening among the lost, to reformation of society and international missionary endeavour. This is the historic path of renewal. We must consciously move toward it in each generation.

When I look at the cities of the United States, I see the Christians as a group of bewildered survivors going about their daily business with little sense of unifying purpose.

In a time of war, battles are won by the strategic concentration of force. Soldiers don't just attack along a scattered front. They follow a plan designed by a general with a big map and lots of information. In some of our cities, it's so long since our soldiers received news about the progress of the battle that they have stopped shooting. They are wandering around the battlefield, preparing food and generally attending to their own comfort.

Nehemiah 4:20 says, "Wherever you hear the sound of the trumpet, rally to us there. Our God will fight for us." The Israelites rebuilding the walls of Jerusalem had knowledge of what the enemy was up to and a system for cooperative action, even though they were scattered on the wall and out of each other's sight.

The modern Christian needs to take the General's

written orders—the Bible—and read the description of the battlefield.

Here is a brief summary of some of the truths about the unseen realm revealed in the Word of God that pertain to the destruction of our cities and how to stop it:

1) Satan's kingdom is a limited hierarchy of evil spirits, with order, authority and chain of command.
2) High-ranking, supernatural personalities, referred to as principalities and powers in Ephesians 6, seek to dominate geographic areas, cities, peoples and subcultures.
3) While God's Word tells believers to treat such beings with respect, it also commands us to take captivity captive, to bind the strong man, to plunder his goods and to tear down the rule and authority of the evil one.
4) We, as believers, are given authority to overcome the enemy as a result of Jesus' victory.
5) We must strategically apply God's power based on discernment of the unseen realm.
6) We need to overcome the enemy before we employ other methods of ministry among people.
7) Jesus said, "...Every city or house divided against itself will not stand" (Matt. 12:25). Spiritual authority is present in proportion to the harmony of relationships among believers moving together toward a common goal.

Assuredly, I say to you, whatever you bind on earth will be bound in heaven,... Again I say to you that if two of you agree on earth concerning anything that they ask, it will be done for them by My Father in heaven (Matt. 18: 18-19).

Many believers are familiar with these seven aspects, but too often these truths become just a doctrine to us. Are you living moment by moment electrified by the realities just beyond the reach of your physical senses? The Bible contains allegorical passages, but what it reveals about the nature of the unseen realm is presented as the factual account of the universe from God's perspective.

One day we will put off this veil of flesh through death or rapture. What we then see will fill us with either remorse at our foolish blindness or wonder and joy as familiar realities come into clear focus.

"If then you were raised with Christ, seek those things which are above, where Christ is, sitting at the right hand of God. Set your mind on things above, not on things on the earth" (Col. 3:1-2).

FOURTEEN

Praying in the Presence of the Heavenly Host

"Then I looked, and I heard the voice of many angels around the throne, the living creatures, and the elders; and the number of them was ten thousand times ten thousand, and thousands of thousands. "

Revelation 5:11

The priorities of eternity and the spiritual world should be the realities that dominate our thinking. Are you a Christian in belief but an agnostic in practice? Do you really act as though the heavenly host existed, or are you as earthbound in your thinking as the average secular pagan?

One day you will die. Will you despise the phantoms of the dream you now call reality? Jesus walked through walls in His resurrection body (Luke 24:36-37), because He was the solid object, and the walls were misty and ethereal.

The next time you are in a prayer gathering listen to how the believers pray. In most cases the saints present

137

do not seem to be aware of what is happening in the invisible world.

To address the living God upon His throne is an awesome thing. His power is deployed through the service of millions of angels. When we pray, we do so in the presence of majesty on high surrounded by a great "cloud of witnesses" (Heb.12:1).

Consider these wise words of Solomon: "Do not be rash with your mouth, and let not your heart utter any–thing hastily before God. For God is in heaven, and you on earth; therefore let your words be few" (Eccl. 5:2).

No wonder the Bible also says, "Likewise the Spirit also helps in our weaknesses. For we do not know what we should pray for as we ought" (Rom. 8:26). This does not mean that we are to be timid when we pray. We need to pray "God-sized" prayers. Consider Psalm 2:8, in which the Father was speaking to the Son: "Ask of Me, and I will give You the nations for Your inheritance, and the ends of the earth for Your possession."

The prayer of a human being can alter history by releasing legions of angels into the earth. If we really grasped this truth, we would pray with intensity, and we would pray constantly.

Recently I attended a national prayer conference and was disappointed by the anaemic praying on the first day. I asked the conference coordinator if I could read descriptions of the heavenlies from the Bible. He graciously agreed. After the reading of the Word, we went back to prayer in small groups. What a difference. The room was filled with the roar of intense prayer as earnest saints took up their weapons and fought.

"That guy is so heavenly minded he's no earthly good," says the old cliche. But is it true? It's true enough if applied to somebody involved in a drug-induced religious mysticism. However, it's false when applied to a believer who walks in faith and obedience to God.

The heavenly minded saints of the Bible changed the course of history. Hebrews 11:16 speaks of the heroes of the faith with these words: "But now they desire a better that is, a heavenly country. Therefore God is not ashamed to be called their God, for He has prepared a city for them."

Will you and I be prepared to pay the price for victory over our cities? There is a high price to be paid in personal discipline, prayer and obedience. We will never be willing to take up our cross unless we have looked into eternity and glimpsed the majesty of God's own character and His eternal purpose for humanity. "Jesus. . . for the joy that was set before Him endured the cross" (Heb. 12:2).

What are we living for? Life is short. Too short to be spent in an anxious search for security. We have identity as God's unique creations and security as His beloved children. Now let's take an adventure with God that begins with taking the gospel to the world and extends into an eternity full of surprises.

I once knew a person who lived entirely for the pleasures of the eternal. This most fulfilled, contented person was Elsie, an intercessor, dying of cancer after forty-two years as a paraplegic shut-in. She first wrote to me in 1977, ten years after her beloved husband passed away. She lived alone, yet was never lonely. The presence of Jesus filled her life with joy in the midst of pain.

> They are abundantly satisfied with the
>   fullness of Your house,
> And You give them drink from the river of
>   Your pleasures   (Ps. 36:8)
> You will show me the path of life;
> In Your presence is fullness of joy;
> At Your right hand are pleasures
>   forevermore   (Ps. 16: 11).

Before she died, Elsie revealed to me the secret behind her joy. Here in her own words is Elsie's experience:

> Nine months after my husband went home to be with the Lord, I was given a vision and given my mission in life from Jesus Himself. It was compassion for all people and intercessory prayer. The Holy Spirit taught me and is still teaching me moment-by-moment abiding in Him.
>
> I, Elsie, am nothing more than a sinner saved by grace, but oh, when I know that Christ in me is all that I am not, I feel like shouting HALLELUJAH! He lives and because He lives I, too, shall live eternally in the heavens. Praise His holy name!
>
> In the vision I was shown the glory of God, the Shekinah glory! We shall be clothed in light. I was given a foretaste of heaven and I can truthfully say, earth at its best is a mere shadow of what God has prepared for us.
>
> On earth we see only reflections of the real things above. Even our bodies shall be changed. Oh, great day when we shall be like our blessed, precious Lord!

Elsie's life demonstrated 1 Peter 4:1-2:

> Therefore, since Christ suffered for us in the flesh, arm yourselves also with the same mind, for he who has suffered in the flesh has ceased from sin, that he no longer should live the rest of his time in the flesh for the lusts of men, but for the will of God.

The apostle Paul, writing to the Corinthians after some of the darkest moments of his life went on to pen words similar to Elsie's. He said:

> Therefore we do not lose heart. Even though our outward man is perishing, yet the inward man is being renewed day by day.
> For our light affliction, which is but for a moment, is working for us a far more exceeding and eternal weight of glory, while we do not look at the things which are seen, but at the things which are not seen. For the things which are seen are temporary, but the things which are not seen are eternal (2 Cor.4: 16-18).

To grasp further the reality of the unseen realm, let's look at one aspect of the "things which are not seen" in greater depth: the existence and activities of angels.

FIFTEEN

All About Angels

"Are they not all ministering spirits sent forth to serve, for the sake of those who are to obtain salvation?"

Hebrews 1:14, RSV

It was a clear desert night. We gazed out the restaurant window at the endless stream of lights. Holiday weekend traffic thundered by on a California freeway.

"Where's Matthew?" asked my wife, Julie.

"He went to the bathroom with David," Paul said.

A few minutes later my oldest son David returned, but the youngest, Matthew, two and a half years old, was missing.

We searched the restaurant. We searched the parking lot. After searching a nearby shopping centre we became desperate. Our greatest fear was that he would stumble onto the freeway or the busy streets, all unfenced, on three sides of the restaurant.

I was searching the steep slope on the edge of the freeway when I found him. He was sitting in the dark, just a few feet from the speeding line of cars and trucks.

"Hi, Matthew," I said, trying not to reveal the panic in my voice.

"Hi, Dad," he said. "The man tied my feet up so I sat down."

"What man?" I said.

"A nice man," said Matthew. "See, my feet are all tied up."

I could see nothing on his little feet, but he acted as though he could not move them. And indeed he could not move them until I reached down and caught him into my arms. "Thank God for His angels!" I shouted into the night.

Julie and I should not have been surprised. As teenagers we had both personally experienced the ministry of angels. Julie was on a summer outreach with Youth With a Mission in Zambia. She was nineteen years old, a new Christian on her first foreign assignment. Late one night, feeling tormented by a number of difficult circumstances, she cried herself to sleep. In the middle of the night she awoke feeling refreshed. The Lord opened her eyes to see a guardian angel, a beautiful creature clothed in light. His hair was white and curly and his eyes, luminous. The room was filled with peace.

I had a similar experience the year before.

In 1971 I left my home country of New Zealand to attend a Youth With a Mission training school in Lausanne, Switzerland. It was totally life changing. Speakers like Loren Cunningham, Brother Andrew and Corrie ten Boom filled us with a desire to serve God as missionaries.

The most memorable experience was actually hearing God speak during a small-group prayer for the nations. God called whole prayer circles to different countries. On the days following the end of classes, my fellow students left in teams for exotic places like Morocco, Germany, Spain and Afghanistan, but I could get no clear direction from God.

I was nineteen years old, and I desperately wanted to be a missionary, preferably in a place like Brazil or New Guinea. Three days after classes finished, I decided to go to Germany because I had some knowledge of German, and I had friends on the pioneering German team, but my spirit was troubled.

"Dear God, just show me what country to go to, and I'll serve You there all my life" was the cry of my heart as I prayed through that day.

The next morning I awoke with a Scripture reference firmly implanted in my mind. It was Ezekiel 3:5. I had never read the Book of Ezekiel, so I had no idea of its content. I read, "For you are not sent to a people of unfamiliar speech and of hard language, but to the house of Israel."

Throughout that morning I listened to God. He spoke to me through portions of Scripture and spoke directly into my mind. To my surprise, He called me to the last place I would have considered for missionary service: the United States of America.

I was so convinced of this direction that I packed my bag and took local buses and trains west across Europe toward the United States. I had twenty-four dollars to begin the trip. My young travelling companion, going as far as England, had little more.

The first night I ended up in a guest house in Darmstadt, Germany. I crawled into bed late at night but I could not sleep. A terrible fear invaded my soul. "What am I doing? My money is half spent. I'll never make it. Nobody knows where I am." All of a sudden a tall, beautiful person was standing beside my bed in the moonlight. "Do not be afraid. I am with you," said a voice that filled me with peace. Then he disappeared. I knew it was an angel of the Lord.

The rest of my journey to the United States was filled

with faith, joy and miracles. This trip became my foundational experience of proving God, but that's another story.

Consider now the following list of facts about angels. I have included references for your further study. As you read and meditate on the implications, let these truths really sink in. You are in the presence of angels right now as you read.

---

1) There are many millions of angels (Rev. 5:11).
2) They are immortal spirit beings created by God to represent and guard His interests (Ps. 148:5).
3) Angels were created some time before the creation of human beings (Job 38:7).
4) Angels are able to manifest themselves in human form, as occurred in the story of Lot and Sodom (Gen. 19; Acts 10:30).
5) Occasionally an angel is revealed in his full heavenly glory (Dan. 10:6; Matt. 28:3).
6) They are spoken of in the masculine gender but do not marry or reproduce. They are a company rather than a race (Matt. 22:30; Luke 20:34-36).
7) Different categories of angels represent different functions and levels of authority, including thrones, dominions, seraphim, cherubim, arch–angels and guardian angels (Col. 1:16; Jude 9).
8) Angels worship before the throne of God and serve Him obediently (Ps. 148:2; Heb. 1:6).
9) Guardian angels are assigned to each child at birth and minister to that person throughout life [except in the event that the person hardens his or her heart against God and determines to do evil] (Matt. 18:10).
10) Angels celebrate before the throne of God every time a sinner comes to God in repentance (Luke 15:10).

11) Angels escort the soul of a Christian to paradise at death(Luke 16:22).

12) Angels record the good and bad deeds of our lives in a book which will be opened at the occasion of the last judgment (Mal. 3:16; Rev. 20:12).

13) Angels are commissioned to execute divine judgment upon persons, cities and nations (Eccl. 5:6; Ezek. 9:1-6; Ps. 35:4-6; 2 Kin. 19:35; Acts 12:23).

14) Angels are used by God to bring messages to people (Zech. 1:9, 13-14, 19).

15) Encounters with angels are usually brief and formal, designed to enhance our relationship with Jesus rather than distract us from Him (Rev. 22:8-9).

16) The Bible warns people not to worship angels (Col. 2:18; Rev. 19:10).

17) Angels now enjoy a superior position to human beings, but they will eventually serve under redeemed humans in the form of the bride of Christ. The bride of Christ is positioned next to God, becoming the elite of all creation (Rev. 21:9-14; 2 Tim. 2:12).

18) Redeemed people will one day judge angels (1 Cor. 6:3).

19) Angels and Christians are allies in the conflict in which they fight to eject Satan from his position in the earth's atmosphere. Prevailing intercessory prayer brings more powerful angels to hinder Satan's work (Heb. 1:4; Dan. 10:12-13).

20) The work of angels is distinct from that of the Holy Spirit. Angels administer material affairs while the Holy Spirit reveals the mind of God. Jesus was led by the Spirit, taught of the Spirit and filled with the Spirit, but He was defended and fed by angels (Matt. 4:11).

21) Some angels are assigned to a specific earthly

territory. The Bible states that Israel and its cities are under angelic guardianship. In Daniel 12:1, Michael is represented as the prince of Israel. The prophet Ezekiel records hearing God speak to angels with these words: "Let those who have charge over the city draw near" (Ezek. 9:1).

Since Israel is a forerunner used to demonstrate God's truth to all the earth, it follows that all nations, cities and subcultures have guardian angels assigned to them. The call that Paul received to Macedonia in Acts 16:9 was evidently communicated by an angel operating in that territory. Peter had a parallel experience with an angel in Acts 10:30.

SIXTEEN

Territorial Spirits

> *"For by Him all things were created that are in heaven and that are on earth, visible and invisible, whether thrones or dominions or principalities or powers. All things were created through Him and for Him. "*
> Colossians 1:16

At the fall of the human race, Satan gained a mandate to become "the god of this age" (2 Cor. 4:4). But since the birth of the church at Pentecost, there has been an ebb and flow of satanic power in specific places at specific times. He is like a squatter that the legal owner of a building must evict.

In human history it is easy to see the enemy coming in like a flood and the Lord raising up a standard against him. In a global sense, each generation faces Satan in the form of the spirit of antichrist or world domination. This is the spirit behind those who have had ambition to rule the world such as Napoleon or Hitler. They would usurp the place that belongs only to

God. "The earth is the Lord's and all its fullness" (Ps. 24:1). A praying church should face this spirit and drive it off long before we find ourselves in a world at war.

Physical violence represents an encroachment of spiritual violence into the material realm. The spirit of world domination can emerge only when the saints have lost their vigilance or when the international church has become severely divided over some issue. Nahum 2:1 says, "He who scatters has come up before your face. Man the fort! Watch the road! Strengthen your flanks! Fortify your power mightily."

It is possible to trace through history the story of battles over states, provinces, cities and neighbourhoods. Consider this example from my experience.

Several years ago I was in a Bible school in New Jersey, browsing through some books on the history of missions to Africa. I began to read the story of Uganda. Many of the first missionaries died of tropical diseases, but others followed heroically until a powerful national church was established.

What caught my attention was an account of the tribal king who dominated Uganda. He was proud, sexually depraved and extremely cruel. The description was remarkably similar to the newspaper reports of the dictator ruling Uganda at that time. Idi Amin and his regime of death seemed to match his predecessor in every detail.

Since that time I have studied the history of Uganda in greater depth. The cycle of blood bath, followed by revival, followed by blood bath is evidence of the ebb and flow of battle, as the national church has come against the evil spirit that prevails over the nation.

South Africa provides another example. Apartheid is a spirit, not just a political phenomenon. It is a spirit of tribalism and of racial separation that goes deep into African history. Apartheid has its roots in idolatry. When a good thing like family heritage is made into an idol, injustice results. A spiritual victory must overcome this ancient oppression.

How do we shatter the power of the spirit behind apartheid? The key is in yielded rights and humble servanthood. We can rebuke the devil all day long and still be powerless unless faith and obedience are strategically applied.

Once I preached to a large, multiracial audience in the Durban Convention Centre in Natal, South Africa. I spoke on the sin of unrighteous judgment and closed the message by leading the people in repentance over racial stereotypes and prejudice. The application of the message later that day was a mass foot washing. Everybody present washed the feet of somebody of another race. Afrikaner, Zulu, Indian, English and those of mixed race wept in each other's arms as a spirit of reconciliation spread across the convention floor.

This may seem like a small victory, but remember that positive political reformation will only grow out of territory gained in the unseen realm. God's promise is: "If My people who are called by My name will humble themselves, and pray and seek My face, and turn from their wicked ways, then I will hear from heaven, and will forgive their sin and heal their land" (2 Chr. 7:14).

I have spent the last eighteen years in extensive travel doing the work of a missionary-evangelist and teacher with Youth With a Mission. I have experienced firsthand the influence of territorial spirits while ministering in over thirty countries.

Often when I first arrive in a new location, I discern the unseen realm most clearly because I sense the contrast in atmosphere between the old location and the new.

For instance, I recently travelled from Belo Horizonte, Brazil, to conduct meetings in Manaus, Brazil. Belo Horizonte is a large city in south central Brazil with many dynamic and growing churches. The pastors of the city have a remarkable degree of unity. Belo is an Antioch, a city with a gift to lead out and to send out. In fact, on that particular trip I had been speaking at a large conference where eighteen Brazilian missionaries were being commissioned for service in Africa.

In Belo you can sense victory in the heavenlies. Like all Brazilian cities, it is young and raw and filled with desperate problems, but the church is alive, and positive changes happen daily.

Manaus is also a large city, set in the jungle, one thousand miles up the Amazon River. Shortly after we arrived, we went to visit Youth With a Mission's base on the bank of the river. It was hot, so I went for a swim, then lay sun bathing surrounded by the tropical beauty of the forest. That night I was to speak at a service downtown, so I stilled my heart before the Lord in preparation. I asked the Lord consciously for discernment regarding the "strong man" or territorial spirit over Amazonas and Manaus.

My senses told me I was in a placid, beautiful place, but the Spirit of God showed me that Manaus was oppressed by a dominating, contentious spirit. That night I preached on discerning the gates of your city. The Lord gave me a word of knowledge concerning this city in some detail. Operating under this principality were spirits working in the fear of authority, distrust, covenant breaking, sensuality, sorcery, greed, despair, regional pride, boasting and religious tradition.

I talked to the Christians about the temptations they must resist: becoming scattered, withdrawn and isolated; losing heart concerning their future; becoming judgmental toward authority figures; walking in polite but superficial relationships. That night two missionaries poured out a story of personal trial that matched exactly what the Spirit of God had revealed to me.

This principle works just as well in the technological culture of North America.

In the summer of 1982 I joined gospel recording

artist Keith Green on his last concert tour of America. (He died in a plane crash that same summer.) We were best friends and enjoyed learning from each other.

The first concert was in Houston, Texas. Before the concert we had a discussion about spiritual warfare and then prayed fervently. Keith was amazed at the results. There was a marked increase in the number of people who came forward during the altar call.

The next night we spent considerable time in spiritual warfare before going to the concert venue. This time the city was Memphis, Tennessee. As we prayed we discerned spirits of religion and apathy as the principalities at work in that city. We turned the concert into a giant worship service. Then Keith turned all the house lights on and preached on commitment to God and repentance from dead works. Again the response at the altar was enormous.

The next concert was in St. Louis. Again we asked God for a specific strategy. That night 631 young people ran to the front to get right with God. The key was to discern the gates of the city, to bind the strong man and then plunder his goods (see Matt. 12:29).

All over the world, praying Christians are arriving at a consensus about the nature of the battle for individual cities. For example, the prayer warriors of London believe that they are battling a spirit of unrighteous trade that has influenced the world through that great city for hundreds of years.

The Bible usually identifies an evil spirit by its territory or by its prime characteristic, for example, "The prince of the kingdom of Persia" (Dan. 10:13) or "Then Death and Hades were cast into the lake of fire" (Rev. 20:14).

We associate New York with mammon, Chicago with violence, Miami with political intrigue. Getting the exact name of demons at any level is not necessary, but it is important to be aware of the specific nature or type of oppression.

Let me add a strong warning. The Bible is a carefully edited book that reflects the priorities of God for the believer and shows us the nature and character of Father God as revealed in Jesus. Although there are many Scripture passages that teach us about the devil and his devices, they are few in number compared with the space given to God's own character and ways. Even good angels are peripheral to the mature believer who is preoccupied with the majesty of the living God and Jesus, His Son.

Very little is revealed about specific territorial spirits in the Bible, and that's no accident. Daniel mentions the prince of Persia and the prince of Greece, and there are New Testament references such as Paul's struggle "with the beasts at Ephesus" (1 Cor. 15:32). However this should not be taken as a mandate for the development of spiritual maps in which we seek knowledge for the sake of knowledge. God will reveal what we need to know when we need to know it.

There has always been a danger of either denial of satanic activity altogether or of focusing on it too much. If we gain knowledge of the name and nature of an evil spirit and publish it broadly, the enemy will only attempt to glorify himself openly or to instil fear among the immature. Joshua warned the Israelites about this temptation. "You shall not make mention of the name of their gods" (Josh. 23:7).

Morbid fascination is a carnal appetite that can drive us to search out the hidden knowledge of the evil realm. The Bible says in Romans 16:19, "I want you to be wise in what is good, and innocent in what is evil" (NAS). True, God reveals hidden mysteries to His close friends. "The secret of the Lord is with those who fear Him" (Ps. 25:14). However, the privilege of knowing God Himself should be the centre of our desire.

Territorial spirits are not responsible for the cultural and geographic divisions within the human family. God Himself claims to be the author of human diversity.

> And He has made from one blood every nation of men to dwell on all the face of the earth, and has determined their preappointed times and the boundaries of their habitation, so that they should seek the Lord, in the hope that they might grope for Him and find Him, though He is not far from each one of us (Acts 17:26-27).

From a biblical standpoint the diversity of human culture comes first from the unique characteristics of individuals and families, such as the traits of Noah's three sons or Israel's tribal divisions stemming from the sons of Jacob. This is a direct result of God's participating in the formation of individual children in the womb. "Before I formed you in the womb I knew you" (Jer. 1:5).

The second major reason for human cultural division also stems from a direct act of God. "Therefore its name is called Babel, because there the Lord confused the language of all the earth; and from there the Lord scattered them abroad over the face of all the earth" (Gen. 11:9).

Modern languages must have developed from the ancient linguistic divisions that came into being when God directly created a diversity of languages at the tower of Babel. The people didn't evolve, learn or develop these root languages. They just started speaking them as God placed new vocabularies within their mouths.

Language is the foundation stone of human cultural division. It's small wonder then that missionary anthropologists like Don Richardson have been able to document the redemptive analogies lying dormant even in the Stone Age peoples of Irian Jaya. In his book *Eternity in Their Hearts* (Regal), Richardson records how God has prepared cultures in every corner of the earth to receive the gospel.

Although God is the originator of human personality and therefore of cultures, Satan has assigned a hierarchy of principalities, powers and rulers of darkness to specific territories on the earth. In this way Satan has marked the culture of every people on earth with some of His own characteristics.

Ancient peoples were profoundly aware of territorial spirits. They gained identity from them and lived in constant fear of them. I believe that most of the ancient gods are still worshipped in other guise by today's secular societies. We teach our children about Greek mythology in school, but we are actually instructing them in the doctrines of an ancient religion that was a matter of life and death to the ancient Greeks. The gods on Mount Olympus were not just literary figures but powerful demons holding the minds of the people in a potent deception.

The cultures of the West are built on a Graeco-Roman foundation. The fundamental beliefs of those ancient cultures are still central to the popular commercial culture of America and Western Europe. By this I do not mean to say that we are consciously bowing down to ancient gods by name. Rather we live out life-styles that have their root in ancient religious practice. Study the ancient Greek idea of success or beauty or personal identity, and you will discover a set of beliefs that are being propagated at the movie theatre down the street.

It is easy to see the demonic in animistic tribes in Africa or the dark fanaticism of resurgent Islam, but do we see the spiritual roots of the modern urban culture of the West? Judeo-Christian revelation has profoundly influenced the institutional life and laws of the West, but the majority of Western people still march to the ancient drums of carnal desire. They march after a life-style dream devoid of the revelation of the one true God.

In recent times the old gods have begun to show their faces again, particularly in children's entertainments. The next time you go to the shopping centre, look through the shops selling comic books and role-playing games such as "Dungeons and Dragons." You will see ancient cultic deities packaged alongside fictional characters in the plot lines of the games and stories. There are also examples of this in teen rock culture and Saturday morning cartoons on television.

In some parts of the world this has moved beyond fantasy. People are again openly worshipping the old territorial spirits. An example would be the renewed worship of Thor and Odin in Scandinavia and the reemergence of the druids in Britain. When you see these signs of satanic influence, be concerned but don't be discouraged. Fear is the enemy's tool and has no place in the heart of the believer. God has plans for your city, and He is the almighty One who cannot be hindered, except by our lack of obedience.

Daniel 7:14 speaks of Jesus' final victory over all the earth's cultures:

> To Him was given dominion and glory and
> a kingdom,
> That all peoples, nations, and languages
> should serve Him.
> His dominion is an everlasting dominion,
> Which shall not pass away,
> And His kingdom the one
> Which shall not be destroyed.

We are to go to prayer with high praise on our lips, not a complaint about the apparent power of the adversary. Read carefully this mind-blowing Scripture: "...to the intent that now the manifold wisdom of God might be made known by the church to the principalities and powers in the heavenly places" (Eph. 3:10). We are to proclaim that the apparent victory of Satan at the cross was really a defeat for him and his ruling spirits. The gospel is bad news to demons and good news to human beings. The cross took away the devil's power of accusation. The cross was Satan's most humiliating mistake.

There is no reason why we, the church, should concede one square inch of this planet to the government of territorial spirits. This is our planet. "The heaven, even the heavens, are the Lord's; but the earth He has given to the children of men" (Ps. 115:16).

Through Jesus we have regained our stewardship of the earth.

> Behold, I give you the authority to trample on serpents and scorpions, and over all the power of the enemy, and nothing shall by any means hurt you.
> Nevertheless do not rejoice in this, that the spirits are subject to you, but rather rejoice because your names are written in heaven (Luke 10:19).

SECTION FIVE

INTO BATTLE:
FIVE STEPS TO VICTORY

*"Be strong and of good courage;
do not be afraid, nor be dismayed,
for the Lord your God is with you
wherever you go. "*
Joshua 1:9

SEVENTEEN

Worship: The Place of Beginnings

"Oh come, let us worship and bow down; let us kneel before the Lord our Maker. "
Psalm 95:6

The strongholds that bind our urban populations have power, but they are not invincible. They're vulnerable, and, if we move wisely, we can overthrow them. This section lays out a fivefold approach to bringing down our cities' strongholds. They are: worship, wait on God, identify with the city's sin, overcome evil with good, and travail until birth.

Everything begins with worship. Everything born of God goes through a very natural process: worship, conception, gestation, travail and birth. So always begin with worship. It's in the place of thanksgiving and praise that God conceives within us His mind and heart for our city.

In the days of King Jehoshaphat, God demonstrated the significance of worship in spiritual warfare by defeating Judah's enemies through the singing of praise instead of through direct military action.

> He appointed those who should sing to the Lord, and who should praise the beauty of holiness, as they went out before the army and were saying:
> "Praise the Lord,
>   For His mercy endures forever."
> Now when they began to sing and to praise, the Lord set ambushes against the people of Ammon, Moab, and Mount Seir, who had come against Judah; and they were defeated (2 Chr. 20:21-22).

The New Testament Greek word for worship, *proskuneo*, means "to kiss toward," implying a deep emotional response toward God. Our heartfelt expressions of praise are rooted in the discipline of thanksgiving. To be grateful is consciously to acknowledge our debt to another, and this is an activity that we are commanded to choose: "giving thanks always for all things to God the Father" (Eph. 5:20).

The opposite behaviour—murmuring and complaining—is a sin that God will not tolerate. Such conduct poisons the atmosphere, robs others of their faith and produces death and defeat. When the children of Israel murmured against Moses and Aaron, 14,700 of them were smitten with a plague and died (see Num. 16:49).

We may know that it's wrong to touch God's anointed leadership, but we often think it's acceptable to murmur against the city we live in because it is inanimate and impersonal. But what was at the root of the people's complaint?   The issue was their environment. "Moreover you have not brought us into a land flowing with milk and honey, nor given us inheritance of fields and vineyards" (Num. 16:14).

What is your attitude toward your city? Most Christians indulge in habitual complaining about traffic, air pollution and other petty annoyances. They fail to realise that reacting to the environment in this way will darken their spirits and stifle the revelation that God wants to bring. Revelation only comes to the grateful because gratitude is evidence of humility. On the other hand, murmuring is evidence of unyielded rights.

I remember the first time I saw Los Angeles in 1971—a vast cityscape smouldering in the summer heat. My soul yearned for the crisp, clean beauty of New Zealand, the land of my birth. The smog burned my eyes and the depersonalising atmosphere of the city pushed down on my spirit. I was happy to leave for Europe a few weeks later, but the dynamic of the city had already captured my imagination.

In 1974 my wife and I spent the summer ministering in Spain and Morocco, after attending the Lausanne International Congress on World Evangelisation. We had been on the road for two years. We had been organising summer outreaches in several countries and preaching on Canadian and U.S. campuses during the school year. Now as we considered the future, God directed us back to the United States and to Los Angeles in particular. We wanted to put down roots, to make disciples, but I approached the city with mixed feelings.

On the one hand, I was excited by the dynamic diversity of the city and its potential as a force for world evangelisation. However, I also struggled with the call to invest my life far from the pleasures of the great outdoors. In New Zealand it was my joy to hunt and fish and climb mountains. My soul took delight in the beauty of nature. Could I now find an equal joy in the urban landscape?

I had an attitude problem toward the city. I took my first steps toward it only out of obedience to Jesus, but God soon changed my perspective.

As I exercised the discipline of thanksgiving, I began to receive constant revelation about the blessings of urban living and the destiny that God had in mind for my city. Now I really love this city. The freeway is a magic carpet ride to new ethnic neighbourhoods, museums, shows and restaurants. The cultural diversity is stimulating, and the vast size of the city provides the opportunity for endless exploration, endless discovery of the new.

The most beautiful thing about this city is the presence of the people of God. I regard it as a holy privilege to be part of the church in Los Angeles. It is a church that has blessed the world with Christian leadership for more than a hundred years. My heart identifies with the rich history of Hollywood Presbyterian Church and also with the newest Pentecostal congregations planted among Central American refugees.

Having to leave Los Angeles now would be a great sacrifice. This is my town. I'm not just passing through while pursuing my career goals. Jesus may relocate me, but unless He directly intervenes, my commitment is not negotiable.

My relationships are more important than my potential for personal achievement. I get angry when I see families leave their local church and all their old friends simply for financial advancement. The prophet Isaiah pronounced God's judgment because of similar attitudes in his generation. "The highways lie waste, the wayfaring man ceases. He has broken the covenant, He has despised the cities, He regards no man" (Is. 33:8).

Are you as excited about your city as I am about mine? Or are you just enduring in an environment that you despise? If you lack joy, repent for your murmuring and then exercise the discipline of thanksgiving. As gratitude conceives praise, you will be able to look up and see the eternal purposes of God for you, your family, and the church in your city.

If you are negative and downcast, you will never minister to this generation. Our primary mission is to bring hope to a generation that is so discouraged that they cannot conceive of anything more than the fleeting pleasure of their vices. Our message to modern humanity is "God is not mad at you! He has provided cleansing and healing through Jesus Christ! Come back to the Father. There is a purpose for your life. "

It is impossible to bring this message unless you yourself are full of the joy of the Lord. "Do not sorrow, for the joy of the Lord is your strength" (Neh. 8:10).

No longer join with Satan, the accuser of your city, but lift up your heart in thanksgiving as you declare by faith the effect that the gospel will have.

> Sing, O daughter of Zion!
> Shout, O Israel!
> Be glad and rejoice with all your heart,
> O daughter of Jerusalem!
> The Lord has taken away your judgments,
> He has cast out your enemy.
> The King of Israel, the Lord, is in your
>   midst;
> You shall see disaster no more.
> (Zeph. 3:14-15)

Do you want revival in your city? Do you want to defeat the powers of darkness? The way to get rid of darkness is to turn on the light, to establish the Lord's presence in the midst of His people through praise (see Ps. 22:3).

It's one thing to have God's strategy for the city, but it's another thing to have God's presence within the people attempting to minister. When Solomon completed the temple according to its design, there still remained the most important event of all. God's glory needed to be manifest in the midst of united praise.

> Indeed it came to pass, when the trumpeters and singers were as one, to make one sound to be heard in praising and thanking the Lord, and when they lifted up their voice with the trumpets and cymbals and instruments of music, and praised the Lord, saying:
> "For He is good.
> For His mercy endures forever,"
> that the house, the house of the Lord, was filled with a cloud, so that the priests could not continue ministering because of the cloud; for the glory of the Lord filled the house of God (2 Chr. 5:13-14).

At the beginning of the Olympic Games Outreach we organised a huge international praise gathering in a stadium. Christians from nearly every church in the city were joined by believers from over thirty countries, until a crowd of sixteen thousand filled the bleachers.

It was not a concert. It was not a time for preaching. It was a time to minister to the Lord, to praise the One who is the only hope of humanity. The infield was filled with people waving banners, each one dressed in a national costume. A full choir and orchestra led us in song, and the evening culminated with the arrival of teenage runners who had carried a lighted torch from Plymouth Rock to Los Angeles, in order to claim the United States for Jesus. "Every place on which the sole of your foot shall tread shall be yours" (Deut. 11 :24).

We were filled with the Holy Spirit and with joy as we celebrated a victory already gained. The days that followed saw an unparalleled harvest.

The people in that stadium were not participating in a choreographed religious frivolity. Each one had been choosing to worship in the lonely moments of personal trial, but now in concert with thousands of others they could pour out their souls in adoration of the Saviour.

That was the night the enemy was defeated. That was the night when the lights turned on and the darkness fled. That was the moment when all the prayers of the previous months found their answer.

Reading a report like this may produce in some people a sense of failure. You may be struggling with the stress of daily living, wondering if your life will ever count for anything, let alone bless a whole city. Don't be discouraged. Start where you are. Remember spiritual warfare begins on a personal level and escalates through increasing levels of difficulty and scope:

- Personal

- Family

- Church life

- Church in the city

- National

- International

All the great victories of the church were conceived in a quiet moment of sacrificial praise, when the heart of an individual turned toward the Lord and worshipped Him for His character alone. Thank God for Himself. Thank God for the privilege of knowing Him, then thank Him for your life and the basic provision of what is needed.

Sometimes I am overwhelmed with gratitude for God's mercy to me. If it were not for His mercy, I would be destroyed. Yet He has given us more than salvation.

He has given us a gift with which to serve our generation.

The more you lift up your eyes in praise, the more revelation you will receive about your destiny. God does not demand praise as an exercise of His own rights. He loves you. When He commands us to give thanks, He is really saying, "Look up, acknowledge Me, and then you will understand."

"The fear of the Lord is the beginning of wisdom" (Ps.111: 10).

EIGHTEEN

Waiting on the Lord for Insight

"Oh, that My people would listen to Me, that Israel would walk in My ways! I would soon subdue their enemies, and turn My hand against their adversaries."
Psalm 81:13-14

Wait on the Lord for insight. Don't rely on finite reasoning or human cunning. Spiritual battles are won by following revelation given by the Holy Spirit. If we listen to God with childlike dependency, He will guide us into victory.

The Scripture is full of exhortations about waiting on God. Psalm 40:1 says, "I waited patiently for the Lord; and He inclined to me, and heard my cry." We are promised that God will speak if we seek Him. John 10:27 says, "My sheep hear My voice...and they follow Me."

Every six months my staff and I gather for three days of prayer. We come together from five different bases located in our metro area. We rarely invite a guest speaker. It's just a time to wait corporately on the Lord. There is a distinct sense of the governing presence of Jesus. We as leaders yield control to the Holy Spirit, and remarkable things often happen. Can you imagine two hundred people waiting on the Lord together? Let me describe what it's like:

On the first day of the gathering the leaders met for early morning prayer in my office. The day seemed like any other, but this day would prove to be different.

As soon as we bowed our heads the white light of God's spotlight seemed to flood our hearts with Holy Ghost conviction of sin. Not that any of us were involved in scandalous behaviour. We just saw ourselves in the light of God's true holiness.

Small things loomed large. Our blind spots were revealed. Our immediate response was to rid ourselves of every hindrance through open confession and repentance.

When we prayed with our staff later in the morning, the same spirit of repentance fell on us all, but God required that we as leaders go first in humbling ourselves through the confession of our faults.

A spontaneous cloudburst of worship followed this time of repentance, and then a spirit of prophecy fell on the people like that described in 1 Samuel 19:20.

Everybody was suddenly full of revelation— revelation about a season of awakening coming to our city. People's minds seemed to be filled with images of rain, which is a symbol of revival. Some had visions, while some received Scripture portions about wells, rivers and floods. Others prophesied about a coming time of harvest.

Then there came a sober mood. Some received Scripture verses about the wickedness of our city and God's judgment. Others wept. We knew our city deserved judgment. We began to feel God's broken heart over injustice, child abuse, addiction, pornography and abortion. The hours flew by. The hand of the Lord was heavy upon us.

In the late afternoon, we moved from travail into warfare. We sang songs of battle and cried out to God for mercy and deliverance.

I will never forget one moment. We were singing a Scripture chorus with these lyrics:

> Summon Your power, O God!
> Show us Your strength
> As You have done before, O God!

We were on our feet singing with all our energy when out of the clear California sky came a huge thunderclap that stunned us into silence. Some of us whimpered; others fell to the floor; all had a terrifying sense of the majesty and power of the Creator God whom we were addressing in praise. "And when they had prayed, the place where they were assembled together was shaken; and they were all filled with the Holy Spirit, and they spoke the word of God with boldness" (Acts 4:31).

Out of these days of prayer came a clear picture of the principalities and powers attempting to govern Los Angeles. The Lord exposed the tactics of the enemy and gave us strategies for his defeat. In united prayer we received God's vision for new ministries to the city.

When we wait on the Lord and give Him room to move, He moves. This was an important factor during the Azusa Street revival and is a characteristic of every divine visitation in history.

One of the most wonderful things about our God is that He is the God who speaks. "He who is of God hears God's words" (John 8:47). The Holy Spirit is present in the church, revealing the mind of the Father.

Biblical characters like the apostle Paul demonstrated a remarkable yieldedness to the specific direction of God in conducting their ministries. "And see, now I go bound in the spirit to Jerusalem, not knowing the things that will happen to me there, except that the Holy Spirit testifies in every city, saying that chains and tribulations await me" (Acts 20:22-23).

Jesus is the greatest example. He even inquired of the Father concerning the words He should speak.

> For I have not spoken on my own authority; but the Father who sent Me gave Me a command, what I should say and what I should speak.
> And I know that His command is everlasting life.
> Therefore, whatever I speak, just as the Father has told Me, so I speak.
> (John 12:49-50)

The Bible warns us about the sin of presumption, which is to attempt to extend God's kingdom without His specific direction. After a great victory at Jericho, the children of Israel experienced a painful defeat at Ai because they did not inquire of the Lord; yet they were to make this mistake again and again.

Our own hearts can quickly become deceived into believing that we have a sufficient knowledge of spiritual truth and can safely come up with our own strategies in doing good. Initiative is a good thing. Volunteering for the battle is a good thing, but remember that our enemy is a master of deception. We are no match for him, unless directed by God's Spirit. "I say then: Walk in the Spirit" (Gal. 5:16).

Shortly after the defeat at Ai, the children of Israel were completely deceived by the Gibeonites. They made a presumptuous covenant with an enemy because they trusted their own reasoning. "Then the men of Israel took some of their provisions; but they did not ask counsel of the Lord" (Josh. 9:14).

Our spiritual authority is proportional to our humility and dependence on God. That dependence is demonstrated by looking to the Lord for direction.

> Trust in the Lord with all your heart,
> And lean not on your own understanding;
> In all your ways acknowledge Him,
> And He shall direct your paths (Prov. 3:5-6).

We can make big plans and bold pronouncements, but it is God Himself who gains the victory. He will only bless what He has initiated. I know what it's like to experience miserable failure, because overconfidence and youthful zeal have at times led me into circumstances far from God's plan or God's timing.

The children of Israel once went up to battle without Moses or the ark. Look at the result:

> But they presumed to go up to the mountain top; nevertheless, neither the ark of the covenant of the Lord nor Moses departed from the camp.
> Then the Amalekites and the Canaanites who dwelt in that mountain came down and attacked them, and drove them back as far as Hormah (Num. 14:44–45).

Do you seek God with intensity only when faced with crisis or faced with important decisions? To do so is to abuse the privilege of knowing God. The best place to become familiar with God's voice is in the place of prayer for others. God delights to speak clearly to the intercessor because intercession is an others-centred activity.

During a large conference for youth pastors, I was asked to speak on prayer. Instead of giving a long talk, I organised the pastors into small prayer circles and instructed them to wait on the Lord for specific direction. I told them to pray for the nations, while giving an attentive ear to the promptings of the Holy Spirit.

After forty-five minutes I asked for a brief report from each group. There was a gasp of excitement across the room when the first group shared that they had felt impressed by the Spirit to pray for Turkey. It turned out that all but five groups in that huge room had spent the time praying for Turkey, without any knowledge of what the other groups were focusing on. Calculate the odds of this happening by accident. There are 223 nations in the world.

Those youth pastors knew that they had experienced a miracle that day. They knew that the living God had actually spoken to them personally and directed them in ministry to the nations. Hearing God's voice is one of the greatest privileges we can experience. The fact that He talks to us is more wonderful than the specific things He says; the plans He has for us are so much more exciting than anything we could concoct.

I remember the first time the Lord directed my friends and me to evangelise a whole town. It wasn't a very big place – only fourteen thousand people in an agricultural valley in Arizona. The town was 40 percent Mormon.

The whole plan came out of prayer; in fact we didn't even know the place existed. My wife and I had just moved to Los Angeles. We simply wanted to mobilise Americans into personal evangelism, but we didn't know where to start.

Each day we met with a small team and prayed for two hours for the youth of the United States. The Lord told us to plan an outreach during the next school vacation, but we didn't know where.

One day a team member brought in a letter ad–dressed to anybody in Youth With a Mission. In it a woman in San Francisco told us about the great need for evangelism in her hometown in Arizona. We all prayed, and the Lord confirmed that this was the place to which He was calling us. It was a long distance, but we set off in my old VW van to spy out the land.

We pulled into town the next evening and asked God to show us the "man of peace" whom He had prepared to receive us. One of the guys noticed a Billy Graham film advertised on the marquee of a movie theatre, so we went inside.

At the end of the film a hog farmer named Dale stood up and gave an invitation to accept Christ. We all really liked this guy. We crowded around him, telling him that we wanted to bring young people to do an outreach. He was delighted and invited us home to his farm.

That night we ate well. Afterward we listened to the godly dream that this man had for his town. He was pioneering a new church and he saw great potential for a spiritual harvest, especially among young people.

The next day I visited the pastors of the four other churches in town. Three were humble and open. One was condescending and suspicious. Paradoxically, his was the denomination with the reputation for the greatest spiritual vitality. But he seemed more concerned with trying to rent us the building than with saving souls. That night we drove back to Los Angeles to begin a season of prayer and recruiting.

Five weeks later we returned to Arizona with over fifty young people. Each morning we went door to door talking about Jesus. Each evening we had a rally at a different church building with all the congregations combined.

The weeks of prayer had really paid off. Everywhere we went, we found receptive hearts. In one of the prayer meetings back in Los Angeles, a team member had experienced a vision. She saw a hard asphalt surface surrounded by a barbed wire entanglement. The Lord showed us that the vision represented the spiritual state of the town; we had to plow up the hard ground through intense prayer if we hoped to see anybody come to Christ.

The results of such prayer were wonderful to see.

Every door was opened to us. We talked to people about Jesus on the golf course, in the bowling alley, in the stores. We were even invited by the owner of the local station to debate on the morning radio show. He was an atheist who hoped to demonstrate his intellectual superiority. However, he could score no points, even though we talked until noon for two days in a row. He resisted the gospel, but his wife began to follow Jesus.

At the end of the week the Youth With a Mission outreach participants had to go back to school, but the town was so stirred up by their witness that my wife, Julie, and I stayed on for an extra week of meetings.

It was Sunday afternoon. I awoke from an exhausted slumber with a strange sense of foreboding. The Holy Spirit spoke to me, "Julie has been hurt. " I pulled a pair of jeans over my pyjamas and ran downstairs. I felt the Spirit draw me to the street in front of the farmhouse. I ran as fast as I could, north along the highway. After a quarter of a mile, I saw a dreadful sight through the heat haze on the blacktop. A farmer had blocked the road with his pickup truck, and he was covering a body with a blanket.

Is she dead? I wondered as I gazed at the large pool of blood beneath her head.

"She's been thrown from a horse," said the farmer. "Her head's all caved in, but I think she's still alive."

The following hours were a collage of red flashing lights, sirens and hospital corridors. They could not give hope. They could not promise me anything. After surgery all I could do was wait.

It was now Sunday evening. I knew the people would be in church. I knew they would be praying for Julie. I decided to join them. I was still wearing my pyjama shirt and my blue jeans, but I washed the blood from my arms and drove to the church.

When the pastor saw me at the back, he invited me to speak. I stood in the pulpit in my pyjamas and bare feet and preached on "Jesus, the lover of my soul" with the full force of my faith and my grief.

At 4:30 the next morning, my dad, in his home in California, was awakened by the Lord. "Pray for Julie; she needs healing," said the Spirit of God. At exactly that time, hundreds of miles away in Arizona, all symptoms of severe concussion left Julie, and she fell into a peaceful sleep.

The next morning she was released from the hospital. All disfiguration had disappeared, but a bandage covered a line of stitches on the back of her head. The Mormon man who owned the ambulance company was so amazed he refused to charge us for his services. "It was worth it just to see a real miracle," he said.

That night all the Christians met in the Adventist building, and the Spirit of God was poured out on us all. The presence of God filled the room. People testified to signs and wonders, new converts proclaimed their faith, people exercised the gifts of the Spirit without self-consciousness, and a cloudburst of spontaneous worship erupted from the people. It was like standing in the midst of a great light. Everything else faded away as we were caught up in the wonder of knowing Jesus.

At around 10:00 p.m. I tried to close the meeting, but nobody took any notice of me. I went home to bed while they worshipped on into the night.

The foundational lesson of this outreach was the understanding that Jesus must be allowed to lead if we are to experience victory. In those days we were in our teens and twenties and had very little understanding of the process of planning or management. However, God was able to do wonders among us because we followed Him with childlike simplicity.

In later years we organised outreaches to much larger towns with hundreds of crusade participants, but I will never forget that town in Arizona—the town where we began to hear God's voice, speaking of His heart for the cities.

At this point a troubling question may have arisen in your mind. How do I know it is God who is speaking to me? How do I know it's not just my imagination? I admit that it's easy to talk to yourself in Jesus' name, but there is an unmistakable quality to the voice of the good Shepherd that cannot be duplicated either by our imagination or by Satan, who is disguised as an angel of light.

The key is to seek God until you know Him. He is certainly willing.

> I said, "Here I am, here I am,"
> To a nation that was not called by My
>   name.
> I have stretched out My hands all day long
>   to a rebellious people,
> Who walk in a way that is not good,
> According to their own thoughts.
> (Is. 65:1-2)

The greatest protection against being deceived by the enemy is to become familiar with the voice of the Master through spending time in His presence.

> The sheep hear his voice; and he calls his own sheep by name and leads them out.
>   And when he brings out his own sheep, he goes before them; and the sheep follow him, for they know his voice.
>   Yet they will by no means follow a stranger ... for they do not know the voice of strangers (John 10:3-5).

If you are involved in any form of leadership among God's people, you will learn soon enough that the security of the flock is not based on their confidence in your experience or your intellect. The children of Israel followed Joshua because he was a man who humbly looked to God for direction. "And the people said to Joshua, 'The Lord our God we will serve, and His voice we will obey' " (Josh. 24:24).

There is one basic strategy of spiritual warfare that undergirds all other strategies: do the next thing that God tells you to do.

> "For My thoughts are not your thoughts.
> Nor are your ways My ways," says the
>   Lord.
> "For as the heavens are higher than the
>   earth,
> So are My ways higher than your ways,
> And My thoughts than your thoughts."
> (Is. 55:8-9)

NINETEEN

Identifying With the Sins of the Cities

"Hear the prayer of Your servant which I pray before You now, day and night, for the children of Israel Your servants, and confess the sins of the children of Israel which we have sinned against You. Both my father's house and I have sinned."

Nehemiah 1:6

The other day I was visited by a businessman who had been listening to my teachings via cassette tape. "I don't know how you can have such hope," he said. "This culture is rotten to the core."

How would you answer him? True, wickedness is woven into the fabric of our culture. Is there hope?

The gospel reveals a message of faith, hope and love. Faith is receiving the knowledge of the Father's ability and character. Hope is the expectation of His goodness to me. Love is the experience of intimate affection, the embrace of the Father, His grace poured out. But the promise of the gospel is realised only as human hearts identify with Christ, our great Intercessor, in His ongoing labour of prayer. That is why the intercessor weeps. Like Jesus, he or she identifies with both God and people.

The great intercessors of the Bible all approached God with a sense of shame and embarrassment. They did not come into God's presence to cover up sin but to agree with His assessment of it. They faced with stark honesty the wickedness of the culture around them.

> "For they proceed from evil to evil,
> And they do not know Me," says the Lord.
> "Everyone take heed to his neighbor,
> And do not trust any brother;
> For every brother will utterly supplant,
> And every neighbor will walk with
>   slanderers.
> Everyone will deceive his neighbor,
> And will not speak the truth;
> They have taught their tongue to speak
>   lies,
> Weary themselves to commit iniquity."
> (Jer. 9:3-5)

Intercession is not an escape from reality. Our communication with God must be rooted in the truth—the eternal truth of His holy standards and the awful truth about our society as God sees it. The intercessor experiences the broken heart of God through the indwelling presence of the Holy Spirit. The intercessor also identifies with the sin of the people, because the intercessor has personally contributed to God's grief.

Our God is a God of patience and compassion beyond human comprehension. His torment is poured out through the prophecy of Jeremiah.

> Why have they provoked Me to anger
> With their carved images,
> And with foreign idols?...
> For the hurt of the daughter of my people

> I am hurt.
> I am mourning....
> Oh, that my head were waters,
> And my eyes a fountain of tears,
> That I might weep day and night
> For the slain of the daughter of my people!
> (Jer. 8:19,21; 9:1)

In responding to the broken heart of God, we must identify with the sins of the city in personal and corporate repentance. When Nehemiah prayed for the restoration of Jerusalem, he did not pray for the city as if he were not part of it. He said, "I and this people have sinned" (see Neh. 1: 6 - 7).

Ezra went even further when he said, "O my God: I am too ashamed and humiliated to lift up my face to You, my God; for our iniquities have risen higher than our heads, and our guilt has grown up to the heavens" (Ezra 29:6).

Both of these were righteous men. You may be a righteous person who is not involved in any direct way with the vices present in your city. But there is no temptation that is not common to humanity (1 Cor. 10:13). We can all identify with the roots of any given sin.

Take, for example, the shedding of innocent blood in the act of abortion. You may never have participated in an abortion, but all of us have been guilty of the root sins that give place to such an activity. I can think of five common roots that lead to abortion: lust, the love of comfort, the love of money, rejection and unbelief.

• Lust, because it is often the context for irrespon–sible conception.

• The love of comfort, because the decision to abort is often made simply to avoid the discomfort of pregnancy.

• Love of money, because of a desire to avoid financial sacrifice.

• Rejection, because in her fear of rejection by society or boyfriend a woman's solution is to reject the child in her womb.

• Unbelief, because we discount the existence of a just God who will surely honour a difficult but righteous decision. The voice of unbelief concludes, "If I have this baby, it will ruin my whole life!"

These are struggles common to us all and illustrate, therefore, the basis of honest identification with the sins of our city when we "stand in the gap" asking for God's mercy. Nehemiah and the families with him assembled themselves before the Lord with fasting, in sackcloth and with dust on their heads. Though they were just a remnant, they completely identified with their nation, their city and its history. "Then those of Israelite lineage separated themselves from all foreigners; and they stood and confessed their sins and the iniquities of their fathers" (Neh. 9:2).

When we ask for God's mercy on others, we should never say, "How could they do such a thing?" We know exactly how they could do it, because the potential for the worst evil lies within each one of us, apart from God's saving grace and the life of Christ within us.

God often gives me an objective in prayer and fills me with faith for an answer. I may be praying for one of my children or praying for the city. As I struggle in prayer for others to be released from spiritual bondage, the Lord begins to reveal the depravity of my own heart.

The issues here are humility and honesty. God cannot use an unclean vessel in the place of intercession. "If I regard iniquity in my heart, the Lord will not hear" (Ps. 66:18). First cleansing, then power. "Sanctify yourselves, for tomorrow the Lord will do wonders among you" (Josh. 3:5).

We need to gain a place where not only do we trust God, but God trusts us. "Search me, O God, and know my heart; try me and know my anxieties; and see if there is any wicked way in me, and lead me in the way everlasting" (Ps. 139: 23-24).

When God has tested us and has found a heart totally dedicated to His purpose, then He gives the promise of access to His power. "If you abide in Me, and My words abide in you, you will ask what you desire, and it shall be done for you" (John 15:7). At this point our prayers become effective in releasing great power. "Confess your trespasses to one another, and pray for one another, that you may be healed. The effective, fervent prayer of a righteous man avails much" (James 5:16).

The Holy Spirit prays through us as the divine intercessor "with groanings which cannot be uttered" (Rom. 8:26), but He can only exercise an authority proportionate to the yieldedness of the human vessel.

My own testimony is that the victories of my life have always come in the midst of repentance and confession. During the Olympic Games Outreach I was surrounded by reporters and television cameras from the Christian media. *Christianity Today* and *Charisma* applauded, and I was interviewed many times on Christian TV and radio.

The atmosphere was one of appreciation. People wrote stories about the fact that God was raising up leadership in the new generation and that there was hope for the future. But in the midst of all that—and there was a great victory taking place—I was going through an intense, personal struggle.

I remember one night in particular. I stood in the dark in my own backyard. The black sky matched my mood. I had been struggling with resentment. Now I couldn't sleep because guilt gnawed at my soul. "God, forgive me," I said one more time, but my own best efforts at repentance brought only the ashes of further failure. I knew what I should be feeling. I should be feeling love, and I should be extending forgiveness. But I had to admit the bitter truth: in spite of all my knowledge of right principle, I was failing at the simplest level of my Christian walk. I'd been hurt and disappointed by a friend, and I could not forgive.

I suddenly saw the awesome truth. John Dawson had not become one bit better after all these years of Christian life. Staring at me from the grave was the same vain, selfish person who had come to the cross so many years before. It's no use putting cosmetics on a corpse, teaching it a new behaviour and a new vocabulary. No one knows how wicked he or she is until that person has truly tried to be righteous.

"God, rescue me," I prayed. "Rescue me from myself." A familiar theme invaded my understanding: the cross of Jesus, His life for mine, the indwelling Christ. Yes, I have always believed that Jesus lives within a believer. But that night in my despair I saw my total need for His life to be the only explanation for any victory of mine. That night I came back to the cross. I experienced again His cleansing and forgiveness. The consequences of my sin had fallen upon the Lamb that was slain. The blood was again sprinkled on he doorposts of my heart. Instead of perfecting righteousness in me, He who is righteous was standing up within me and beginning to live His life.

Jesus is the only person who can truly live the Christian life. That night with a new understanding, I acknowledged again my total dependence on Him. We are by nature incomplete. Human beings by definition are the dwelling place of God. God has created us as a vessel for His own being. In a sense, we cannot be fully human apart from Him.

Jesus doesn't dispense His attributes to us as we need them. He doesn't give us *some* love. He is love. His life unleashed within us is the source of all victory and blessing. He is everything that I am not. He is consistently loving, completely honest and quick to forgive. My only hope is consciously to acknowledge my desperate need of Him. "Jesus, live Your life through me" has become my daily prayer.

My biggest problem is not demons. I am my biggest problem. It is only when God has cleansed my own wicked heart that participation in the redeeming work of intercession becomes possible. It is then that the power to change history is released through prayer.

> Elijah was a man with a nature like ours, and he prayed earnestly that it would not rain; and it did not rain on the land for three years and six months.
> And he prayed again, and the heaven gave rain, and the earth produced its fruit (James 5:17-18).

As you stand in the gap for your city, allow the Holy Spirit to shine the bright light of truth into the inner rooms of your soul. Run from the religious deceit that would seduce you into believing that you are superior to any person. It is only by the blood of the Lamb and the power of the Spirit that we stand free from the chains of guilt and the sentence of death.

> Woe is me, for I am undone!
> Because I am a man of unclean lips,
> And I dwell in the midst of a people of
>   unclean lips;
> For my eyes have seen the King,
> The Lord of hosts (Is. 6:5).

TWENTY

Overcoming Evil With Good

"And they overcame him by the blood of the Lamb and by the word of their testimony. "　　　　*Revelation 12:11*

Is the enemy tempting us to be fearful and stingy? Let's come against greed with hilarious generosity. Overcome pride with humility, lust with purity, fear with faith, lethargy with diligence. Paul said, "I can do all things through Christ who strengthens me" (Phil. 4:13). Overcoming evil with good is not merely a spiritual technique, but represents a means of applying the victory of Jesus already gained.

Satan's kingdom seems to employ a principle of reversal. He delights to reinforce his power over people by tempting them to do the opposite of what is natural. Such practices as homosexual acts or even the sacrifice of children sear the conscience and bring people into Satan's control through condemnation. To live in truth involves turning an upside–down world right side up.

Resisting Temptation

When we come against the enemy, we by faith manifest the aspect of Christ's character that is the opposite of the temptation facing us.

Take, for instance, Jesus' statement regarding a particular evil spirit. "However, this kind does not go out except by prayer and fasting" (Matt. 17:21). The admonition to abstain from food is probably because the disciples were dealing with a demon of appetite such as lust or gluttony. The power of God was hindered until they yielded themselves further to the control of the Holy Spirit through a particular step of obedience—a step involving the opposite spirit, a spirit of self-control.

Fasting, however, has a greater significance as a means of overcoming the enemy. Fasting is intensely difficult and sends us running to Jesus for help. When your body is screaming for food, you know you need grace to go on. Denying your appetite becomes an intense personal battle. Hunger and weakness humble me. I desperately need grace to maintain my commitment to abstain from food. The poverty of my self-sufficiency is exposed, and Christ's sufficiency is revealed instead.

The application of the cross always releases resurrection power. We are crucified with Christ, and our old nature is destroyed. Then Christ's life inhabits our life in victory. This is the principle of the exchanged life: His life for mine, His strength perfected when I acknowledge my weakness. "It is no longer I who live, but Christ lives in me" (Gal. 2:20); "for without Me you can do nothing" (John 15:5).

Coming against Satan's strongholds always involves personal choices that overcome temptation. Temptation serves the purpose of exposing what is really in our accident was clearly the other person's fault. They told me that a judge would have to decide that. I was escorted to prison to await trial.hearts. When we see what is in our hearts and acknowledge it honestly before God in repentance, His greater power is released.

When we have discerned the activity of a principality with a particular characteristic, we need to cultivate the opposite characteristic, not only through resisting temptation but by demonstrating positive action.

Taking Positive Action

Let me give you an example from my own life. Someone once said that "to the early church, Christianity was a faith, the Greeks made it a philosophy and the Americans have made it an enterprise." No place is this more evident than in Southern California where I live. The mammon-dominated culture founded during the gold rush has dramatically influenced the way Christian organisations function. The Bible says that the kingdom of God does not consist in buying and selling, but in giving and receiving. The kingdom is not advanced through the cunning principles of trade but through love and trust in relationships.

In 1985 I began to give copies of our large mailing list of forty thousand names to any worthy group with a kingdom cause. I did this as a deliberate act of spiritual warfare, because I wanted to strike at one of the lies that Satan uses to bind the church in my city. He manipulates us through the fear that our needs will not be met. Mailing lists are one of the prime assets owned by Christian organisations. They are groomed, guarded and looked to for survival. In freely giving away the list I had a firm conviction that I was overcoming the lust for control in my own spirit. I was declaring to Satan that we would break his stronghold over the city in this area and move from jealous competition to loving co-operation.

I experienced the most dramatic example of the opposite spirit principle when I overcame fear with faith in the Juarez jail. For several years we had been ministering in Mexico. One of our greatest problems was dealing with the fear of corrupt and abusive elements within the Mexican federal police.

On this particular occasion we were full of faith, "prayed up" and ready for evangelism as we approached the Mexican border through the city of El Paso, Texas. I was leading a group of around fifty YWAM students on a school field trip. We had a school bus, two lorries, a van and a travel trailer in our convoy. We were equipped and provisioned for two months in Central Mexico. As we began to cross the border, disaster struck. I was about to experience some of the most terrifying days of my life.

God allows Satan's attacks for three reasons:

• The Lord wants to build character in us.

• He wants to expose and defeat the enemy.

• He wants us to occupy territory for the kingdom which was once held by the powers of darkness.

Satan comes against us as a roaring lion, seeking to devour us. But in every attack the Lord allows, a blessing is in store for us.

I had an accident at the border crossing. My lorry and trailer were impounded; my staff and students went back into Texas. Included in the group were my wife and our baby boy who now had no place to stay.

I was taken to the police station and informed that there was a serious problem. One of the customs booths had been damaged in the wreck, and under Mexican law there was a minimum two-year sentence for damaging government property. I told them that the accident was clearly the other persons fault. They told me that a judge would decide that. I was escorted to prison to await trial.

In those days, there were two prisons in Juarez: a relatively modern one and an ancient, colonial fortress notorious for its harsh conditions. As we drove to the old prison, the policeman apologised that the other one was full. He warned me about what I would face. Fear gripped my heart.

One of the students had given me some passages from the Bible. As I looked down at the crumpled scrap of paper in my hand, I read:

> My soul is among lions;
> I lie among the sons of men
> Who are set on fire,
> Whose teeth are spears and arrows,
> And their tongue a sharp sword (Ps. 57:4).

> Every word of God is pure;
> He is a shield to those who put their trust
>   in Him   (Prov. 30:5).

The prison was much worse than I had imagined. It was a walled compound. The guards patrolled the top of the walls with machine guns but did not dare to enter the prison itself except as a fully armed posse. There was no food or water provided except through relatives of the prisoners, so in order to live those who had nothing fought with those who had something.

A pecking order of criminals controlled the prison. One of their scams was a protection racket to extort bribes from other prisoners. Because I was a gringo, it was assumed that I had money, so I was taken by a crime chieftain to a cell with twelve other inhabitants. Each man paid the mob twenty-two U.S. dollars each week for the limited protection of an enclosed space.

The prison was a seething cauldron of fear. Murder was common; homosexual rape was rampant; drugs were used openly. I had no money and nothing with which to protect myself. No watch, no wedding ring—only a Bible, pants, T-shirt and a pair of flip-flops. As soon as I entered the cell, a big Mexican tried to steal my flip-flops. The only way to keep them was to keep standing on them.

The Lord spoke to me very clearly. "Your weapons are not carnal, but spiritual. Move in the authority I have given you as a man of God. Minister the gospel to them. This will be your protection."

I asked if anybody spoke English and was soon in conversation with a professor from Juarez University who had been convicted of embezzlement. "God has put me in here to tell you something," I said, and I proceeded to tell him of the Father's love.

Several hours later the mob realised that I had no money. They pulled me out of the protection cell and threw me into the snake pit. The snake pit was a huge room filled with men who were the lowest of the low. The insane, the violent, the most promiscuous of the homosexuals. I was surrounded by a mass of tattooed, semi-naked, leering men. They looked like demons inside human skins. A powerfully built boss criminal parted the crowd, sized me up and claimed me for himself.

There were tiny wooden cubicles built up the side of the walls. He escorted me to his and told me that from now on I would sleep there as his personal property.

The men jeered at me and decided to have some fun. They made me clean the floors with an old rag, like a slave. After some time I was approached by a Chicano from Los Angeles. He had a simple message for me. "This is hell. Do what you have to to get out. If you can't get out, kill yourself. It's the only way. Some of us have been rotting in here for years without any due process of law." I assured him that I was innocent and would soon be released. He just laughed. But I had my Bible; the Chicano was a good interpreter, so I began to tell everybody about Jesus.

That night, just as things were getting really dangerous, an amazing thing happened. The professor whom I first witnessed to was so hungry for the gospel that he paid my bribe. He spent his own protection money to get me out of the snake pit and back into his cell. I was even more happy to see him than he was to see me. We spent the next two days reading the Bible together. Then I was released to the judge for trial, and the professor, having spent his bribe on me, was taken to the snake pit. That man had always feared the snake pit, but his hunger for the good news was greater than his fear.

I was eventually proven innocent and released. Our outreach to Central Mexico proceeded as planned. In the process, I was a changed person. I was completely delivered from fear of the Mexican authorities. In exercising faith in the prison, I had received a love for the police and a burden for prisoners. Galatians 5:6 says that faith works through love. I had learned that fear is really faith in the devil, faith in a person or faith in yourself.

That first night in the prison, I lay on the cold cement floor with bronchitis, facing two years of unjust confinement, but I was being guarded by the Prince of Peace, the authority above every other authority in Mexico. I was in the worst possible circumstance. The enemy had fired his fiery darts at my hidden fears, but it only became an occasion for God to reveal His greatness.

I spent the rest of the summer boldly entering the Mexican prisons and preaching the gospel. I knew the territory. It belonged to Jesus and me.

But You, O Lord, are a shield for me,

My glory and the One who lifts up my
    head.
I cried to the Lord with my voice,
And he heard me from his holy hill.
I lay down and slept;
I awoke, for the Lord sustained me.
I will not be afraid of ten thousands of
    people
Who have set themselves against me all
    around (Ps. 3:3-6).

Think about your city.

• What is oppressing you and your neighbours?

• What positive actions could you take that resist the
enemy in his strongholds?

• What are you responsible for?

• Are you a pastor?

Your church has been commissioned to rip up the
evil roots from past sins that have given place to Satan.

Do you have a building project at the church? If you
do, it may not be just a building project but an
opportunity to conduct spiritual warfare over the whole
city. The collection of offerings for a new sanctuary, for
example, can be an occasion to break strongholds.

Is there a spirit of greed rooted in your city? This is
often the case where a city first prospered through
mining, like Denver or Johannesburg, or through trade,
like London or Hong Kong.

Take up that first offering and give it to another
church. Take up the second with shouts of joy. Provoke
the congregation with the big picture—the plans and
purposes of God for the whole city. Move them beyond
themselves. If we build the church through simply

appealing to them to build facilities for themselves and their children, we are just another enterprise trading in goods and services.

I know of congregations who have experienced years of delay with property development. It's time to discern what is hindering and to intensify prayer and action against it. One of the names of God is *Baal Perazim* meaning "Master of Breakthroughs". Daniel didn't give up. He kept praying for twenty-one days until revelation reached him.

Perhaps your church is oppressed with apathy. Prophesy against it and lead the people in high praise.

Is the congregation exclusive and religiously proud? Join with that other church of poor folks on the other side of town for a service or two.

Are they afraid of evangelism? Get mad at the devil's lie and lead them into evangelism. "He who is in you is greater than he who is in the world" (1 John 4:4); "I am God... I am He; and there is no one who can deliver out of My hand. I work and who can reverse it?" (Is. 43:12-13).

Creating With God

Along with resisting temptation and taking positive action, there is always the release of God's power when we declare out loud His *rhema* word. The Greek word *rhema* is the biblical term for the specific personal communication of God with His children here and now. This is different from the *logos*, which refers to the already revealed word recorded in Scripture.

Since Pentecost, we have become the dwelling place of God's Spirit. God wants us to think His thoughts, pray His prayers, feel His heart, do His work and speak His words.

Because we are the legal stewards of this planet, it is important for a human being to speak out an authorisation for action on the part of angels. The non-

Christian has lost his authority and is under the prince of this world (John 12:31), but the redeemed believer has regained the right of dominion (Gen. 1:28). The accuser can no longer condemn. The blood has been sprinkled on the doorposts (Ex. 12:23). Judgment has already fallen on the Lamb. The curse is broken. He has delivered us from the kingdom of darkness and transferred us to the kingdom of His dear Son (see Col. 1: 13).

Within our right of dominion is the privilege of speaking into existence the purpose of God as He reveals His mind to us. "But we have the mind of Christ" (1 Cor. 2:16). In this way we create with God new things and destroy the works of darkness. We speak in the name of Jesus, through the power of the Holy Spirit, because of the shed blood of Jesus with the sword of the Spirit which is the Word of God.

The Bible does not depict us as passively sheltering but as consciously fighting. James 4:7 says, "Therefore submit to God. Resist the devil and he will flee from you." Matthew 18:18 says, "Whatever you bind on earth will be bound in heaven."

Several years ago I was in a plane approaching Burbank airport in California. Suddenly the plane began to buck and lurch violently. I was about to tell my wife and children that airplanes were safe, and the problem would soon be solved when the voice of the Lord cut into my thinking. "Take authority over this plane," He said.

I understood immediately. With quiet intensity I spoke out these words: "This plane will safely land; Satan and demons, you will not hinder us; the problem will be resolved in the all-powerful name of Jesus right now. We are children of the most high God, conducting our Father's business. So I commandeer this plane in the authority of the almighty God and command it to set us safely on the ground!"

After more severe gyrations, the plane landed

awkwardly and was immediately surrounded by nine fire trucks. I can still remember vividly the sensation of looking out the window into the brass nozzle of a foam gun, held by a man in an asbestos suit. The crew hurried us off the plane and, to this day, I don't know themselves what the true situation was. All I know is this: there is a time for me to die, but that was not it. It was important to God that I exercised my will and spoke with my mouth, and that I consciously invoked the higher authority of God in speaking to the mechanical or human problem facing that airplane that day.

There are many occasions when I have spoken to my city, just like Zerubbabel shouting, "Grace, grace!" in bringing forth the capstone (Zech. 4:7). I often pray when driving on the freeway. "God will be glorified in this city! " I shout. "Jesus' power is greater than the violence and despair in the streets, greater than the apathy and division in the church. This city will see an awakening. 'Thanks be to God, who gives us the victory through our Lord Jesus Christ' [1 Cor. 15:57]. Satan and demons, you will not have this city. This city belongs to Jesus and will yet fulfil its destiny in bringing blessing to the nations."

I never say these things flippantly or as a religious invocation. I don't even see these words as a product of my own intellect and imagination. During times of intense prayer the Spirit of God sometimes moves on me to proclaim boldly the intent and purpose of God's own heart.

Unfortunately, Satan also understands and uses this principle. Seers, mediums and fortune-tellers affect the very future they pretend to know by predicting events. When they make the declaration, they unleash spiritual forces to bring about such things as accidents or assassinations. This explains the power of curses and many of the counterfeit signs and wonders of demonic religion.

We have nothing to fear however. The Bible says, "A curse without cause shall not alight" (Prov. 26:2), and "No weapon formed against you shall prosper" (Is. 54:17).

Consider the words of this psalm as a summary of the truth we have just discussed:

Let the saints be joyful in glory.
Let them sing aloud on their beds.
Let the high praises of God be in their
    mouth,
And a two-edged sword in their hand.
To execute vengeance on the nations,
And punishments on the peoples;
To bind their kings with chains,
And their nobles with fetters of iron;
To execute on them the written
    judgment—
This honor have all His saints.
Praise the Lord! (Ps. 149:5-9).

TWENTY-ONE

Travailing Until Birth

"So it was, when I heard these words, that I sat down and wept, and mourned for many days; I was fasting and praying before the God of heaven." Nehemiah 1:4

Just as the contractions of a woman's uterus herald the beginning of labour, there are times when God's Spirit stirs our souls to seasons of intense travail. We must travail in prayer until God's purposes are birthed. This may be an exercise that is deeply personal and private or a corporate exercise, for example, as part of scheduled citywide prayer meetings. That which is conceived of God will eventually come to birth. When the united Christians of a city are at this stage, it is an indicator of impending revival.

When you truly love somebody, you don't just mention that person before the Lord. You pray *until* that which is needed happens, until the answer comes, until breakthrough. Love settles for nothing less than victory. Love fills us with an earnest ambition for the desired result.

If you are praying for a family member who is in bondage, you are not released from the burden until that person is saved, set free and set in order. This is the way we should pray for our cities. "Ask, and it will be given to you; seek, and you will find; knock, and it will be opened to you" (Matt. 7:7).

In the year prior to the Olympic Games Outreach, I would often find myself groaning and weeping with the compassion of Jesus for the people of my city. I drove the freeways with tears streaming down my face. Later that year, hundreds of pastors from over fifty denominations joined with me in times of intense prayer during outreach planning sessions.

There will be seasons in the life of every intercessor. The process of physical birth is an analogy of an eternal truth. A woman is incapable of bringing to birth a great many children in a short time. She must endure through a certain process which then produces the promised child in the fullness of time. The year 1983 was one of intense travail in my personal prayer life for my city. I was totally consumed by the struggle to receive that which God had promised.

The level of a spiritual victory for your city is directly affected by two spiritual conditions: the intensity of your desire and the size of your faith. God wants to see if you want the minimum or the maximum. Do you want institutional survival or citywide revival?

The prophet Elisha took the young king Joash to a window facing east. Elisha instructed the king to fire an arrow in the direction of the Syrians and then to act out his zeal for victory.

> Then he said, "Take the arrows"; so he took them. And he said to the king of Israel, "Strike the ground"; so he struck

three times, and stopped.

> And the man of God was angry with him, and said, "You should have struck five or six times; then you would have struck Syria till you had destroyed it. But now you will strike Syria only three times." (2 Kin. 13:18-19)

Moses did not make this mistake. His life as an intercessor was marked by intensity and endurance. Moses was also a man who had his personal priorities sorted out. It is recorded in Exodus 18 that his father-in-law, Jethro, taught him that intercession for the people was the first of the six responsibilities of leadership.

This list based on Exodus 18:19-22 has been immensely helpful to me, and I keep it prominently posted on the front page of my prayer diary:

"Stand before God for the people" (intercession, the number one priority).

"Teach them the statutes and the laws" (prepare key teachings).

"Show them the way in which they must walk" (long range vision).

"And the work they must do" (the plan, how we get there from here).

"Select from all the people able men, such as fear God" (appoint leadership).

"Every great matter they shall bring to you" (keep your energy for the truly important things).

The pastor of a church or the leader of a ministry will find it difficult to maintain these priorities, because prayer is essentially private. It is the one aspect of a leader's ministry that is invisible to the people. We are easily tempted to a life of ceaseless but barren activity, because we want the approval and understanding of the people who follow us. We must repent of the fear of man and ask God for a life-transforming revelation of the priority of prayer.

Most of us learn to pray with intensity through concern for our children. God's main method of turning a self-centred teenager into an others-centred adult is to set us in families.

The principle is this: the grace for character transformation is always a love relationship. Think of the story of Jacob. He spent fourteen years of indentured servitude learning to hate his own character weaknesses as he saw them reflected in the life of his manipulative uncle Laban.

Why did he stay and endure this painful learning experience? Answer: he was in love with Rachel. In Genesis 29:20 the Bible reports the astounding grace this love provided: "So Jacob served seven years for Rachel, and they seemed but a few days to him because of the love he had for her."

Love for Rachel sustained Jacob during the difficult season of his apprenticeship for leadership. Eventually his name was changed from Jacob, which means "supplanter or schemer", to Israel, which means "prince of God".

We rarely anticipate the surgery that God intends when we fall in love, marry and produce a family. It reminds me of a mischievous friend of mine who would always change the words of a popular worship chorus and sing, "Grind us together, Lord, grind us together, with cords that cannot be broken. "

When we are single we long for the intimacy of marriage—just to have somebody of "my own". We fantasise about moments of emotional and physical intimacy. Eventually we may get married and face the reality of actually dividing our time, money and space with another person. That's when we discover how much we really need Jesus.

And then come children. Tiny, smelly, little creatures that demand constant attention. Ah, but what love fills our hearts at first sight of Baby. Our selfish focus on personal rights is swept away the moment those big baby eyes look into ours.

When a baby is born into a family, the parents virtually become its slaves. We clean them, feed them, warm them, protect them and sometimes we do it all night long.

During the years of their early childhood, our major concern is for the physical safety of our children. That is often the focus of our prayer life, but then they reach their teens. The day my oldest son entered secondary school, I knew that my prayer life would have to change. Now I can truly identify with Paul's statement in Galatians 4:19, "My children with whom I am again in labour until Christ is formed in you" (NAS).

God, our Father, uses the experience of parenting to help us to identify with Him. The Holy Spirit speaks to us about sharing our faith with others; but most Christians approach evangelism with a heavy heart and a fear of rejection, even though a twinge of guilt reminds them that their obligation is plain.

Why do we share Jesus with others? Why do we pray for people? Because people need Him? Because we look at strangers and simply love them so much? Because of duty and obligation?

If you love someone, you will seek to comfort that person and help him or her at the point of greatest hurt. We have a brokenhearted Father who has entrusted us with an awesome responsibility and privilege: the expression of His love to a hurting generation.

Jesus said, "As the Father has sent Me, I also send you"(John 20:21). Our very name is the "body of Christ." This means that our hands must become His hands, our eyes shine with His love and our voices speak His words. As His people we represent Jesus to the world. Where else will they see Him?

I have three children. I love to hold them, comfort them and teach them. I cannot imagine what it would

205

be like to have no arms to hold them and no voice to comfort them when they experience pain. God has entrusted us with the awesome privilege of expressing His heart of love to His own wayward children. How vulnerable God has made Himself to us! We cannot fail His trust. We cannot ignore His broken heart over millions who still walk in ignorance of His plan of reconciliation.

We often hear preachers talk about a ministry of reconciliation. Evangelism is literally that, but when you see a stranger walking down the street, you don't immediately love that person. Indeed, you can't love that stranger.

Have you ever wondered what it feels like to have a love for the lost? This is a term we use as part of our Christian jargon. Many believers search their hearts in condemnation, looking for the arrival of some feeling of benevolence that will propel them into bold evangelism. It will never happen. It is impossible to love "the lost". You can't feel deeply for an abstraction or a concept. You would find it impossible to love deeply an unfamiliar individual portrayed in a photograph, let alone a nation or a race or something as vague as "all lost people".

You may have read the testimony of praying missionaries who wept with loving compassion for the people of their calling. However, don't forget that this experience is a result of God's emotions being shared with a human heart in the place of intercession. God does not relate to commodities and abstractions. In His omnipresence, He knows and relates to individuals. He does not see a conglomerate, such as the nation of China, as much as He sees every Chinese person, whom He has known intimately since conception.

Don't wait for a feeling of love in order to share Christ with a stranger. You already love your heavenly Father, and you know that this stranger is created by Him, but separated from Him, so take those first steps in evangelism because you love God. It is not primarily out of a compassion for humanity that we share our faith or pray for the lost; it is, first of all, love for God. The Bible says in Ephesians 6:7-8: "With good will doing service, as to the Lord, and not to men, knowing that whatever good anyone does, he will receive the same from the Lord, whether he is a slave or free."

Humanity does not deserve the love of God any more than you or I do. We should never be Christian humanists, taking Jesus to poor sinful people, reducing Jesus to some kind of product that will better their lot. People deserve to be damned, but Jesus, the suffering Lamb of God, deserves the reward of His suffering, which would be that none perish, but that all are reconciled to the Father.

When you do open your mouth to testify to others as a love response to God, the indwelling Christ will reveal His tender heart. The apostle Paul testified to this motivating work of the Holy Spirit. "For the love of Christ constrains us" (2 Cor. 5:14).

When we minister to people either through prayer or through preaching, we must give the Holy Spirit access to our emotions. Many Christians are unable to move with the Spirit into seasons of travail because they have a fear of experiencing deep emotions. The root of this hindrance is the fear of losing control, yet our whole spiritual life depends on our yielding control to the Holy Spirit.

God has promised that if we follow Him, He will remove our hearts of stone and give us hearts of flesh. The suffering that once made us so bitter is now the crucible in which compassion is forged. "For as the sufferings of Christ abound in us, so our consolation also abounds through Christ" (2 Cor. 1:5).

The only thing that will sustain the intercessor through a long season of prayer is continual revelation from the Holy Spirit. The Spirit loves the Father; the Spirit reveals the Father's compassion; and the Spirit gives us the faith to know that the joy of answered prayer will always come to those who continue in faithfulness.

One of my first experiences of learning to pray until breakthrough was as a result of picking up a hitchhiker late one night. He was about eighteen years old, lonely, miserable and strung out on drugs.

I offered him a place to stay and a meal and talked to him about his heavenly Father. At one point in our conversation I felt such compassion for this young man that I didn't know if my heart could endure it. I said, "Colin, God has loved you since the day you were born. He has longed for somebody to tell you how much He loves you. He understands you. He knows about every hurt and every disappointment. When you cry, He cries."

Something stirred deep within his young heart. He looked at me with such longing, but he was unable to respond to the Lord that night. He had taken too much speed to sleep, so he continued his journey.

In the months that followed, my schedule took me to several countries, but the Lord had planted a seed of compassion within me for Colin that grew into a greater burden as time passed. The Holy Spirit would direct me in very specific prayer. I remember calling on God for Colin's deliverance from drugs while I was driving through a Canadian snowstorm. I remember rebuking demons of sexual perversion during a prayer time in Osaka, Japan.

The day I returned to Los Angeles I was greeted by an excited Youth With a Mission worker. "Colin got saved," he said.

"Which Colin?" I said, guarding my hopes.

"Some guy you picked up hitchhiking. He got saved today, just before you got here," he said.

When I opened the front door of the Discipleship Training School, there he was, tears in his eyes, surrounded by students who had just led him in the sinner's prayer.

He had been in a nearby park dealing some dope when he looked through the trees and recognised the Youth With a Mission property. He remembered the kindness of the Lord to him, threw his drugs into a trash can and stumbled across the street weeping.

When a staff member responded to his knock at the door, he said, "I want to come in. I need to get saved." And of course he was welcomed into the family of God.

During my months of prayer for Colin, I was amazed at the Holy Spirit's ability to move my emotions. I had only talked to him briefly, but a supernatural energy for prayer was awakened within me. If Christ "ever lives to make intercession for them" (Heb. 7:25), then we must receive by faith this aspect of His life even as we have received His cleansing and His victory over sin. Christ's prayer life must be expressed through us by the indwelling Holy Spirit.

In 1971 I was a student in a Youth With a Mission school of evangelism in Switzerland and I was just beginning to understand spiritual truths. One day Loren Cunningham called a special prayer meeting for the United States, and several of us joined him in an upstairs room.

The first thing he did was to invite the Holy Spirit to deal with sin. I came under deep conviction because of my judgmental attitude toward others. I confessed this openly and gained great joy immediately.

As people prayed for the United States, the Spirit directed me to a particular subculture. "O God," I prayed, "reveal Yourself to the rebellious children from Christian homes who are now living in counterculture communes in San Francisco. "

Immediately after saying these words, my whole body was racked with deep sobbing. I was unable to pray another prayer. I remember thinking: how can I feel so deeply for people I have never met, living in a country foreign to me? It was my first experience of

Jesus, the Intercessor, sharing with me His burden for lost people. I could feel their loneliness and confusion. I sensed what it would be like to bear a mountain of unresolved guilt, to live under the accusations of tormenting spirits.

The Holy Spirit suffers continually as He enters into people's pains and sorrows. Through the Spirit the intercessor makes the suffering of others his own. Intercession is not a substitution for sin—that is the finished work of Jesus through the cross—but the intercessor completely identifies with the sufferer in his physical or spiritual condition. This outworking of divine love gains the release of divine power.

Love is measured and demonstrated by sacrifice—by costly action. Love continues no matter what the cost. "Greater love has no one than this, than to lay down one's life for his friends" (John 15:13). Love identifies with suffering and endures until it is ended. Paul said,

> Now if we are afflicted, it is for your consolation and salvation (2 Cor. 1:6).
> ...always carrying about in the body the dying of the Lord Jesus, that the life of Jesus also may be manifested in our body.
> For we who live are always delivered to death for Jesus' sake, that the life of Jesus also may be manifested in our mortal flesh.
> So then death is working in us, but life in you (2 Cor. 4:10-12).

The patriarch Abraham received a promise from God, but then he travailed for a lifetime in receiving its fulfilment. "And so, after he had patiently endured, he obtained the promise" (Heb. 6:15).

We, too, need to endure until that which God has promised us is completed. Sometimes just hanging in there can be an act of spiritual warfare. You must endure in the circumstance until the character of Christ is formed in you, and you gain that needed place of spiritual authority.

Resurrection power comes only after the cross has done its work. Self-interest, self-promotion, self preservation and self-consciousness have to die for us to experience intimate friendship with a holy God and to obtain overcoming authority in destroying the works of Satan.

No victory is instant. I have a friend who once filled her home with needy people, many requiring deliverance from demonic oppression. She rushed from person to person, counselling and comforting until she was completely exhausted. She commanded demons to depart but continuing bondage was evident.

Finally she became oppressed herself and even entertained thoughts of suicide. In this dark moment God taught her that deliverance is a process.

She turned her home into a house of prayer. Each person received counselling only when she felt that a place of authority had been gained through intercession. Some victories were quickly gained, but others required seasons of intense struggle.

I remember an early example of this principle in my life. I was standing before a large film screen in a Canadian high school auditorium. Colourful posters had been posted throughout the campus, inviting students to attend a lunchtime meeting.

Christian students had invited many of their friends, and we were expecting a large crowd. We anticipated good results through the sharing of a powerful gospel film featuring youth issues.

At the time the film was due to begin, only a handful of students had entered the auditorium. I was discouraged.

I went around behind the screen and paced up and down praying fervently. "Lord, bring them in. Holy Spirit, sweep down the corridors and draw students to this room. Bring them to an appointment with the Father today."

I kept this up for fifteen minutes without any visible result. The accuser tormented me with my failure, and I almost packed up my equipment and left. Then it happened. Students began to pour into the room. Not just Christians. Students of every style and persuasion.

Finally there were no more chairs, and students began to line the walls and sit on the floor. I stayed behind the screen and kept on praying. "Every one, Lord, every person who needs to be here, bring them in."

A line formed in the corridor outside the auditorium. A frantic school teacher began turning people away because the room had become so crowded that we were violating the fire code.

Behind the screen I was weeping and worshipping. "Forgive me, Lord, for not trusting You. I see now that You move in great power if I press in for the maximum result. Complete the work today, Lord; complete the work."

In the meeting that followed, God changed many lives.

Thirty minutes of earnest prayer is barely a valid example of honest travail, but the Lord had to start me somewhere. In the years since then I have travailed for months or even years over people and ministries that the Lord has laid upon my soul. He has graced me with a stubborn faith that contends for the promise and does not let go.

Ezekiel was given this holy stubbornness when God commissioned him to the ministry of a prophet.

> Behold, I have made your face strong against their faces, and your forehead strong against their foreheads.
> Like adamant stone, harder than flint, I have made your forehead; do not be

afraid of them, nor be dismayed at their
looks, though they are a rebellious house
(Ezek. 3:8-9).

We need the humility to change direction in an
instant, if we are shown to be in error, and the tendency
to continue against all odds, for as long as it takes to
complete the task that God has assigned to us. This
"holy stubbornness" is particularly important when
praying for breakthrough in a city. Seasons of harvest
will come; new ministries will be birthed. However,
these things will not take place instantly.

God plants within the heart of every believer a godly
dream. But, like Joseph, we find ourselves walking
away from the mountain of promise into the valley of
apprenticeship. Like Jacob we may begin the journey in
human strength, but God must reduce us to an honest
appraisal of our weakness before we can inherit the
promise. Many visions die on the road to resurrection
power. God subtracts before He multiplies.

And the Lord said to Gideon, "The people
who are with you are too many for Me to
give the Midianites into their hands, lest
Israel claim glory for itself against Me, saying, "My own hand has saved me"
(Judg. 7:2).

Paul's testimony must become ours: "I have been
crucified with Christ; it is no longer I who live, but
Christ lives in me; and the life which I now live in the
flesh I live by faith in the Son of God, who loved me
and gave Himself for me" (Gal. 2:20).

I have had to suffer painful failure to learn this
lesson. Fifteen years ago during a staff prayer day, God
gave us a burden for the runaway children who
congregate in Hollywood and San Francisco. Part of the

vision God gave us was for the development of a farm property as a conference centre, a teen camp and a place to give runaways a new start.

The first property we occupied was an old airport terminal next to a tiny farm town, eighty miles north of Los Angeles. This facility was only temporary. We eventually returned it to the Christian developer who owned it.

The next property was located near a resort town in a beautiful mountain valley in central California. There were twenty acres of land and several useful buildings. The property was a gift, and we received it with much rejoicing, but not until much prayer had taken place. We sought the counsel of many wise people and we were convinced that the Lord was guiding us in this step. The Holy Spirit impressed upon us the need to worship in all circumstances, but only later did we realise the significance of this word.

The ministry got off to an encouraging start, but, within a few months, contention and accusation had divided the staff, and the first leader left in discouragement. A new leader was sent from Los Angeles, and he began to rebuild the team. Within a few weeks he ran into great legal complications in attempting to develop the property further. Without new buildings the property had very limited potential. We became bewildered. Why had God led us to this place?

During this time we experienced a tragedy. A little boy named Shawnie Blignaut, the child of one of our staff members, drowned in one of the ponds on the property. The team was devastated. The Youth With a Mission leaders gathered with Christians from the community at the funeral and worshipped with the child's grieving family. The Spirit of God comforted the mourners with a heavenly peace, but it was a death blow to the morale of the team.

The ministry continued for a few months, but

without much enthusiasm. We eventually retreated from that town, grieving over our loss, and turned the property over to another organisation.

I could not understand the failure of this ministry. I had prayed over this project more than any of the others. I had moved in unity with my eldership and those who advise us. I had received many promises from God, but now they seemed to mock me from the ashes of my defeat.

All we could do was worship, to offer to the Lord costly praise. "Be merciful to me, O God, be merciful to me! For my soul trusts in You; and in the shadow of Your wings I will make my refuge, until these calamities have passed by" (Ps. 57:1).

It became a dark night of the soul in which we worshipped God for His character alone without one shred of understanding about our circumstance. "Who walks in darkness and has no light? Let him trust in the name of the Lord and rely upon his God" (Is. 50:10).

All our hopes and dreams seemed to lie in the grave with that little boy, and we had no desire even to look for a new place to start over again. As we continued to worship, God began to build within us an enduring faith that is not contingent upon the measure of our progress, the number of our resources or the strength of our allies. We praised Him as the God who brings resurrection, when all human strength has been expended.

Many months went by. We seldom thought of the original promises God had given us many years before. We were not in unbelief; we just didn't know if we qualified to inherit that which God had promised.

We continued in our ministries in Los Angeles—training missionaries, sheltering runaways, ministering to refugees, organising outreaches. Then one day I received a phone call and was plunged into a surprising set of new developments.

A generous organisation gave us a huge property

with very little debt remaining. Previously the complex belonged to a ministry and, although in need of some repair, it included more facilities than we had ever dreamed of.

A beautiful old hotel sits on five hundred acres of land—surrounded by many houses, repair shops, a lodge, classrooms, a swimming pool and a one–thousand-seat auditorium. We were overwhelmed by the scale of God's plans for us. We had to scramble to staff such a facility. But God had prepared some of our people with the right gifts, and now a thriving ministry is growing in what has become the headquarters base for Northern California. "Those who sow in tears shall reap in joy" (Ps. 126:5).

What is your personal vision? Is there a God-inspired dream burning in your heart? Don't give up. Let God have His way with you. Keep your eyes on the King, receive His vision for the city, give Him your life and your gifts, and begin to take steps of obedience.

None of us understands the end from the beginning. All we know is that He is "the author and finisher of our faith" (Heb. 12:2). God's ways are too marvellous for us. I understand more than I am able to put in this book, but what I do understand is tiny. I live on the edge of wonders beyond my capacity to comprehend. The more my curiosity is satisfied, the more the wonder of knowing God increases.

Like you, I live on a dying planet, a dark place polluted with demons, but growing in my heart is a fierce joy. Sometimes to know God is to experience dread and regret, but most of the time I feel delight and wonder.

God is the most interesting Person in the universe— and the most beautiful. He is gentle and just, infinite and yet personal. Jesus came to reveal the Father, to atone for us and to teach us how to live. He also came to destroy the works of the devil, and He has commissioned us to do likewise.

There was a little city with few men in it; and a great king came against it, besieged it, and built great snares around it.

Now there was found in it a poor wise man, and he by his wisdom delivered the city (Eccl. 9:14-15).

That wise man could be you.

Study Guide

INTRODUCTION

This study guide is to use with the book, to help the members of a congregation apply these truths to daily living.

Even our children can be taught to think strategically; to live for kingdom goals beyond their immediate needs and concerns.

I remember listening to Brother Andrew during a missionary training course in 1971. Even though most of our class consisted of new believers, he discussed the world with us like we were veteran missions executives.

Because we were taken seriously, we began to take ourselves seriously, and many in that class have gone on to establish powerful ministries that have blessed the nations.

It is my prayer that believers everywhere will see their potential to contribute to revival and harvest, and that this guide will give them encouragement and understanding.

John Dawson

Lesson 1

Battle Stories

This lesson covers Chapter 1, "Seventh Time Around" (pages 17-21) and Chapter 2, "The Discerning of Spirits" (pages 23-29).

Notes to the Teacher

The book should be read by each member of the group in advance. These lessons are no substitute for the thoughtful reading of each chapter in private.

As you discuss this first chapter, draw upon the experiences that group members may have had with the supernatural, but bring them back again and again to God's Word and God's character.

There are questions that will be raised in this first lesson which will not be dealt with until later, so stress the fact that you are beginning a journey and that things will come into focus as you continue to examine God's Word together.

Lead the group in a prayerful request for revelation from the Holy Spirit.

I. Introduction

As we raise children, conduct business and pursue the ministries that God has given us, we will face the opposition of the satanic kingdom.

Satan has assigned a hierarchy of wicked spirits to our city and neighbourhood, but we are to see ourselves as warriors rather than victims. Our steps of obedience and faith contribute to a bigger victory than our own.

223

One of the abilities or gifts of Jesus' Holy Spirit within us is the ability to discern the activity of spirits (1 Cor. 12:10).

This book focuses on the deliverance of cities and nations rather than individuals. It is important to note that there are no stories that depict an individual identifying principalities and powers and then singlehandedly overcoming them. This is because God is at work in a sphere bigger than our understanding and He uses us only as a contributor to victory, not as the prime mover, lest any man should boast that he had done the work of God.

II. Claiming This Generation for God

III. Seeing With the Eyes of Faith

IV. The Power of Prayer and Fasting

V. Discerning the Unseen Enemy

VI. Prayer Strategy

****

Spiritual warfare begins at a personal level and escalates through layers of increasing difficulty, from personal and family to the realm of church life and beyond that to the collective church in the city and the national and international realms.

****

Notes to the Student

Questions for thoughtful reflection:

1. What has the Lord already taught you about the tactics of the enemy in your neighbourhood and city?

2. Do you know of any group of believers who are uniting in prayer and outreach to your city?

3. Which ideas discussed in these two chapters are new to you?

4. How intense is your prayer life when it comes to matters beyond your immediate personal needs?

5. Have you ever been part of a Christian outreach or organisation that sought to bring about positive changes in your city?

6. Are you willing to personally apply the truths that you discover during these classes?

Be involved by answering these questions:

1. What did the young people hope to gain by running from the East Coast to the West? (page 17)

....

....

2. Why did the people of Cordoba suddenly respond to the gospel? (page 18)...

....

3. What does the term "bind the strong man" mean to you? (page 20)..

....

4. List the gifts of the Holy Spirit as described in the New Testament...
....

5. What is the purpose of the gift of discerning of spirits?..
....

6. Does the praying believer always fully understand the implications of simple steps of obedience to God?
....
....

7. What happens in the heavenlies when we pray?
....
....

APPLICATION TO DAILY LIVING

Spiritual authority is a by-product of personal devotional habit. One of our greatest privileges is to create with God through the daily practice of intercessory prayer.

Consider these guidelines:

1. Romans 8:26 tells us that we cannot pray effectively without the energy and direction of the Holy Spirit, so ask for God's enabling grace and receive it by faith.

2. Invite the Lord to search your heart and to reveal the things that need to be exposed to Him through honest confession. "If I regard iniquity in my heart, the Lord will not hear" (Psalm 66:18).

3. Refrain from hastily praying out your own ideas. Give God time to share with you the divine perspective. This includes both God's compassion and His wisdom.

4. Pray with fervour and with faith. You are bringing your requests to the Creator of the universe. You are approaching the Father of all mercy.

5. Speak out the promises of God and be alert to the possibility of God speaking to you through a Bible passage.

6. Continue in prayer until you sense a release in your spirit. Don't just mention things to the Lord. Press on until the Holy Spirit has fully expressed the mind of God on the subject.

7. End your prayer with thanksgiving and praise. Thank God for answered prayer, but most of all thank Him for who He is, for His matchless character.

Lesson 2

What Are All These Demons Doing on the Planet Anyway?

This lesson covers Chapter 12, "Born to Battle" (pages 125-131).

Notes to the Teacher

We will cover this chapter of the book in our second lesson, even though it appears halfway through the text, because it will give us a necessary theological foundation. This lesson could even proceed as a Bible study. The group could read and then discuss a series of Bible texts such as those outlined below.

I. Introduction
Before going any further, we need to learn how we came to be on a planet infested with demons, and learn God's eternal purpose for us as revealed in the Bible.

II. What is man supposed to 'subdue'?—Genesis 1:28

III. Who won the war?—Revelation 12:9

IV. If the devil is defeated, why is he loose in my town?— 2 Peter 2:4

V. Does God really want us to learn to fight?
Judges 3: 1 - 2

VI. What is our delegated task?—Psalm 149:8-9

VII. What is God preparing us for?
2 Corinthians 4: 17

****

The development of man in his ultimate potential depended on an experience with an adversary.

****

Notes to the Student

Questions for thoughtful reflection:
1. Are there concepts in this chapter that are new to me?

2. How does this help me to understand God's justice?

3. Do I really understand the wonderful privilege of ruling with Christ in eternity?

4. Have I considered the demonic hierarchy more powerful than it really is?

5. Is this book teaching me how to overcome demons or how to qualify for my inheritance?

6. Who kept Moses out of the promised land, the Canaanites, evil spirits or God?

Be involved by answering these questions:
1. God created man with a free will. Is love possible without it? ....
....

2. What was God's motive in creating humankind?

....

....

3. What was Joseph's final attitude towards his personal suffering? ....

....

4. Has Satan assigned certain demons to certain territories?

Explain...

....

5. What are Satan's two primary weapons against humanity? (page 128)..

....

6. In what way has Jesus empowered us to destroy the works of Satan?...

....

7. Is the authority that Jesus has given us conditional?..

....

APPLICATION TO DAILY LIVING

When we contemplate the wonders of eternity there are so many unanswered questions.

The foundation of our faith is not a comprehensive knowledge of all things. That would be impossible because our minds are finite. What we can know is the unchanging character of the Creator. God has gone to great lengths to reveal Himself to us. The testimony of

Scripture and our personal experiences teach us of God's natural attributes, His personality and His moral character.

Use the following outline as you read the Bible this week.

What does each passage reveal about who God is?

God's Natural Attributes:
    God is....   Infinite
                     All powerful
                     All knowing
                     Omnipresent

God's Personality:
    God is...   Like a loving parent
                     Like a loving husband
....
....

God's Moral Character:
    God is...   Always honest: Truth
                     Always merciful: Love
                     Always fair: Justice
                     Always consistent: Faithfulness
                     Always patient: Self–Control
                     Always choosing
                         the best for all: Wisdom
....
....

Feel free to expand these lists with your own discoveries.

The knowledge of God is the most important education you will ever have.

Lesson 3

What Are We to Do?

This lesson covers Chapter 13, "The Unseen Realm" (pages 133-136) and Chapter 14, "Praying in the Presence of the Heavenly Host" (pages 137-141).

Notes to the Teacher

This lesson centres on living your life in the light of eternity. Our objective is to put our trials and tribulations in perspective and to learn what happens when we pray.

Ask the group to share what they have discovered about God's character through Scripture meditation during the last week.

I. Introduction
The following seven truths pertain to the destruction of our cities and how to stop it. Each concept will be explored in greater depth in later chapters but this will provide an overview.

II. Satan's kingdom is a limited hierarchy of evil spirits, with order, authority and chain of command.

III. High ranking, supernatural personalities, referred to as principalities and powers in Ephesians 6, seek to dominate geographic areas, cities, peoples and subcultures.

IV. While God's Word tells believers to treat such beings with respect, it also commands us to take captivity captive, bind the strong man, plunder his

goods and to tear down the rule and authority of the evil one.

V. We, as believers, are given authority to overcome the enemy as a result of Jesus' victory.

VI. We must apply God's power strategically based on discernment of the unseen realm.

VII. We need to overcome the enemy before employing other methods of ministry among people.

VIII. Jesus said, "...Every city or household divided against itself will not stand" (Matt. 12:25). Spiritual authority is present in proportion to the harmony of relationships among believers moving together toward a common goal.
"Assuredly, I say to you, whatever you bind on earth will be bound in heaven,... Again I say to you that if two of you agree on earth concerning anything that they ask, it will be done for them by My Father in heaven" (Matt. 18:18-19).

****

We will never be willing to take up our cross unless we have looked into eternity and glimpsed the majesty of God's own character and His eternal purpose for humanity.

****

Notes to the Student

Questions for thoughtful reflection:
1. Am I responding to my difficulties like Elsie? (page 139)

2. Is the presence of Jesus in my life the chief source of my happiness?

3. How often do I really think of eternity?

4. If I came face to face with Jesus tonight, would I have regrets about the priorities that govern my life?

5. Do I give lip service to the importance of prayer, but live as though the Bible's description of the spiritual realm is a myth?

6. Do I need to apologise to God for my unbelief and receive cleansing?

Be involved by answering these questions:
1. What does Elsie's life teach me about God's grace?...
....

2. How did the Apostle Peter view suffering? (1 Peter 4:1-2, page 140)...
....

3. Solomon said, "Do not be rash with your mouth..." (Eccl. 5:2, page 138) What was his reason?
....
....

4. How does prayer affect history? (page 138)
....
....

5. What is the relationship between unity and spiritual authority? (page 135)..
....

6. Do God's people have a united strategy to reach my city?..
....

7. What is my contribution?...
....

APPLICATION TO DAILY LIVING

Page 134 contains this statement:

> "The rightly prioritised agenda of a biblical believer should be personal repentance and holy living, leading to united prayer, to revival of the church, to awakening among the lost, to reformation of society and international missionary endeavour. This is the historic path of renewal. We must consciously move toward it in each generation."

Meditate on the implications of this statement. Is it true? If so, how have you directly contributed to this process?

Ask God to reveal to you your next step of obedience.

Lesson 4

All About Angels

This lesson covers Chapter 15, "All About Angels" (pages 143-148).

Notes to the Teacher

Begin by reading aloud the 21 points listed on pages 146-147. If particular points stimulate the curiosity of the group, look up the Scripture references listed in each point and ask for other biblical passages that reinforce the same truth.

Our objective is to inform the group of the function of angels, but even more than that, to cause them to marvel at the privilege of being created in God's own image and destined for the throne.

I. Introduction

How many of us have heard sermons or read books about angels? So much has been written about demons that we sometimes forget that they are completely overshadowed by God's majestic and obedient angels.

II. The function of angels in service to God.

III. The function of angels in service to God's people.

IV. Angels at war.

****

"Are they not all ministering spirits sent forth to serve, for the sake of those who are to obtain salvation?"
Hebrews 1:14, RSV
****

Questions for thoughtful reflection:

1. Am I in the presence of guardian angels right now?

2. Have I ever thanked God for the privilege of being served by angels? (Heb. 1:14, page 143)

3. When I consider the surrounding presence of angels, can I justify my fears?

4. If recording angels preserve the knowledge of my actions, what do I want to erase through confession and the application of the blood of Jesus?

Be involved by answering these questions:

1. Of the 21 facts about angels, which are new to you?...
....

2. What happens in the heavenlies when we travail in prayer like Daniel? ....
....

3. How does the task of angels differ from that of the Holy Spirit?...
....

4. Are some angels assigned to help God's people in specific territories and cities?.......................................
....

5. Is the loyalty of a guardian angel primarily to the person served or to God? ....
....

6. Do all angels have the same function?

....

....

APPLICATION TO DAILY LIVING

The Bible teaches that we will one day rule with Christ over the angelic kingdom. What is it about us that God finds so valuable?

> Is it our righteousness?
> Is it our power?
> Is it our wisdom?

Or is it our beauty? The Bible reveals that our ultimate value is that of the "bride" of Christ. (Rev. 22:17). In God's opinion, we are "fearfully and wonderfully made" (Ps. 139:14), the most beautiful of creation.

Jesus is at work within us creating the beauty of holiness, but He has already created you with a body, personality and giftings that are unique and valuable. This week ask yourself the question, "In what way has the accuser tempted me to reject the way God has created me?"

Lesson 5

Principalities and Powers

This lesson covers Chapter 16, "Territorial Spirits" (pages 149-158).

Notes to the Teacher

This is an area of teaching that must be taught with balance. Cover all the concepts in this chapter, including the warnings on page 154. An increase in knowledge always brings with it the temptation of pride, and the knowledge of territorial spirits can be a temptation to fear.

End this lesson by reading Luke 10:19 and leading the group in a time of thanksgiving and praise for the finished work of Jesus on the cross.

This chapter contains stories about the dramatic results that have occurred when united believers have "bound the strong man" and "plundered his goods" (Matt. 12:29).

In this study, we will be called upon to think big, to pray very specifically in a God-directed way for our city.

I. Introduction

II. Ruling Spirits

III. Our Battle Against Them

IV. Seated With Christ Above All

****

There is no reason why we, the church, should concede one square inch of this planet to the government of territorial spirits.

****

Notes to the Student

Questions for thoughtful reflection:

1. Are the temptations I experience similar to those experienced by everybody else in this town?

2. Has God revealed anything to us about the nature of Satan's oppression here?

3. Have I been in self-pity about the attacks of the enemy instead of rejoicing in God's unfolding plans?

4. Do I act like this city belongs to God and His people?

5. Am I a victim or an overcomer?

6. When was the last time I rejoiced because my name is written in heaven? (Luke 10:19)

Be involved by answering these questions:

1. How did Satan gain his operating authority here on earth?...
....

2. What are some of the manifestations of antichrist or world domination that have occurred in human history?...
....

3. What conditions within the church set the stage for global destruction, such as during WWII? (page 149)
....
....

4. Why has history repeated itself in Uganda? (page 150)..
....

5. Why did the number of people saved in Keith Green's concerts suddenly increase?
Explain:..
....

6. Why should you be cautious about seeking detailed information about specific principalities and powers? (Josh. 23:7, page 154) ....
....

7. Who is responsible for the diversity of human culture? (pages 155-157)..
....

8. Why was the crucifixion of Jesus Satan's most humiliating mistake?...
....

APPLICATION TO DAILY LIVING

Have you ever prayed for anything larger than your own family and circle of friends, something as large as a city? The Bible is filled with examples of people who changed the course of entire nations through intercessory prayer.

God only asks that we do what we can. Like the small boy who brought Jesus his loaves and fishes, we can bring Jesus our small prayers and He, by His power, will surpass our expectations.

Begin to pray for the spheres of influence that shape the citizens of your city.

- Home life and families
- The churches and other religious institutions
- The educational system
- Entertainment and the arts
- City government
- Business and commerce

Lesson 6

Deliver the Dark City

This lesson covers Chapter 3, "A Call to the City" (pages 33-37), Chapter 4, "Cities: A Blessing or a Curse?" (pages 39-45), Chapter 5, "Ministering in the City of the Future" (pages 47-55), Chapter 6, "Revival or Judgment—What Will It Be?" (pages 57-67) and Chapter 7, "The City at Harvest Time" (pages 69-74).

Notes to the Teacher

This lesson covers five different chapters, all dealing with the nature of the urban mission field. Have the five different group members briefly review what they learned from each chapter.

Each of these chapters deals in some way with the sin of unbelief as a hindrance to God's plans. Turn the discussion towards the greatness of God, proclaiming Him as the Lord of the cities.

I. Introduction

Before discussing the ways we advance God's kingdom, we will examine the context of our ministries, the modern city.

II. Jesus is ministering downtown right now.

III. The Accuser of the City

IV. Your city has a redemptive gift.

V. Satan is manipulating the institutions of man.

VI. God is up to something even bigger.

VII. Mega-cities, Mega-opportunities

****

There are millions of Christians who choose where they will live on an entirely self-centred basis. We need Jesus' view. Cities are simply huge clusters of people, and Jesus goes where the people are.

****

Notes to the Student

Questions for thoughtful reflection:
1. Have I thought of my city as dark and evil or have I seen the hand of God at work here?

2. Have I ever pictured what revival would look like in this town?

3. Have I been limiting God by my unbelief?

4. Do I love this city or have I joined with the accuser in my attitudes toward it?

5. Am I praying for a harvest among the youth like the Jesus Movement of the early 1970s?

6. What strata of urban life can I influence most effectively?

Be involved by answering these questions:
1. What is meant by the concept of redemptive gifts?..
....

2. Are there redemptive gifts evidencing them—
selves in the life of your city? List two.

....

....

3. Why did the manager of the pornography shop
finally turn to Jesus? (page 42)...

....

4. Explore the concept of a "communication
village". (page 53)...

....

5. What are the two fundamental steps in spiritual
warfare? (page 73)...

....

6. How big does your city look from the throne of
God? (page 55)...

....

APPLICATION TO DAILY LIVING

After today's lesson you should be seeing your city
through new eyes. Eyes of faith and expectancy, not
fear and cynicism.

Try to picture God creating the geography of the
area long before it was inhabited. Ask yourself why
people built a city on the site.

Ask God for revelation about His plans for revival
and harvest. Ask God for a revelation of His broken
heart.

Right now God is seeing marriages break up, children abused, pastors losing hope, children unloved, those tortured by addiction and a hundred other griefs. For God's sake begin to pray. Redeem the time on the motorway or time spent on repetitive tasks.

Lesson 7

Discerning the Gates of Your City – I

This lesson covers Chapter 8, "Looking at History With Discernment" (pages 77-86) and Chapter 9, "The History of God's People/Covenants" (pages 87-95).

Notes to the Teacher

This could be one of the most interesting lessons, especially if the group is asked to read chapters 8 and 9 in advance and to begin research on the questions posed at the end of each chapter. Let each person share what they have found and then talk about the exciting possibilities of further study.

I. Introduction

Discerning the nature of the enemy's strongholds can be as simple as asking God to tell us what's going on. But God also wants us to learn principles, to reason through the things in His Word and to apply them. Nehemiah carefully surveyed the damaged walls of his city and we need to do the same.

II. We have an enemy who exploits woundedness and corruption (Lord of the Flies).

III. God did not give demons authority over your city.

IV. Sin provides the place of entrance for darkness.

V. Repentance and reconciliation can repair the ancient breaches in the wall.

VI. Where are the walls of my city broken down?

****

"Your descendants shall possess the gate of their enemies." Genesis 22:17

****

Notes to the Student

Questions for thoughtful reflection:
1. Have I succumbed to the spirit of the world around me like the pastor from Reno almost did? (page 81)

2. Can I answer any of the questions on page 83?

3. Is my level of knowledge inadequate for God to use me in effective spiritual warfare? (page 84)

4. Am I willing to join with others in a prayer movement? (page 84)

5. What is the unfinished business of the church here? (page 85)

6. Do I really appreciate the contribution of the church in previous generations? (page 91)

7. Have I expressed deep gratitude to God for all the movements and ministries that have enriched the church in my nation's history?

Be involved by answering these questions:

1. Why is it important to study past revivals?
(pages 87-88)..
....

2. What happened spiritually during the California
Gold Rush? (page 78)..
....

3. Explain what God revealed about how to heal the
wounded spirit of Australia. (page 78).............................
....

4. Name three Christian movements whose history
you know and whose contribution you appreciate.
(page 91)...
....
....

5. Why is it essential that you understand the work
that God has given your church to do ? (pages 92-93)
....
....

APPLICATION TO DAILY LIVING

Pages 83–84 and 91-94 contain lists of important
questions that require much thought and, in some
cases, detailed research.

Research is not everyone's best talent, but to the
degree that God has given you aptitude, pursue the
answers to these questions.

What begins as a project may become a way of life for some of you. Ezra and Nehemiah were guided into their destiny by a profound awareness of the history of their people. Daniel fasted and prayed until God gave him revelation about three things.

We need the same kind of information that Daniel received.

1. Revelation with which to interpret our history.

2. Direction from God concerning today's steps of obedience.

3. Promises concerning the future of our people.

Lesson 8

Discerning the Gates of Your City – II

This lesson covers Chapter 10, "Prophets, Intercessors and Spiritual Fathers" (pages 97-110) and Chapter 11, "Get the Facts"(pages 111 -121).

Notes to the Teacher

The objective of this lesson is for the group to gain appreciation for the diversity of ministries in God's kingdom, and to see how they are orchestrated together under the kingship of Jesus. This understanding should be discussed in the context of today's facts and tomorrow's trends in the city in which you live.

I. Introduction
We have looked at the past to understand the inroads of the enemy, the progress of the battle and the promises of God for our city. Now let us see how to receive the wisdom that God has deposited in the saints of today and how to gather the data that will help us straegise.

II. We need a strategy.

III. What is God saying through His servants?

IV. Is there a team I should join ?

V. The Apiskopos at work.

VI. But do we really know this town?

****

An individual ministry can achieve victory within its sphere, but the prevailing evil spirits will dominate the secular culture unhindered until the principle of agreement, based on harmony in relationships, is employed.

****

Notes to the Student

Questions for thoughtful reflection:

1. If our relationships with one another form the invisible walls of the city and broken relationships can hinder the effectiveness of our prayers, what shape are we in right here in this town?

2. Do I really understand and appreciate what God has called each Christian ministry to do?

3. Do I understand the unique gifting of my own congregation?

4. Is the ministry of our church or organisation properly targeted?

5. Not everyone with a good-sounding plan is expressing God's mind. How will I know who to follow? (page 98)

6. Is my life having any positive effect on the poor and needy of my city?

Be involved by answering these questions:

1. "If a kingdom is divided against itself, that kingdom cannot stand" (Mark 3:24). What are the implications of this statement?...

....

2. Should we organise into one giant structure? (pages 98-108)...

....

3. How has a society of urban commuters affected the life of today's church? (pages 99-102).........................

....

4. Based on your general knowledge, list three trends in your city. (page 115)...

....

5. Which trend represents the greatest opportunity for the gospel? (page 119)...

....

6. Which subculture represents the poorest of the poor, the most vulnerable and needy group in the city?

....

....

7. List two sources of information for research on your city. (page 119)..

....

APPLICATION TO DAILY LIVING

When we have a working knowledge of the city, suburb or country that God has called us to, we are able to receive revelation from God about a specific strategy for ongoing evangelism and discipleship.

This week continue to research the needs and opportunities around you, but give particular thought to the four directives listed in chapter 10.

1. Know the church, its movements and the ministries given to people.

2. Listen for the sound of the trumpet. "He who has an ear, let him hear what the spirit says to the churches" (Rev. 2:7).

3. Receive God-given gifts of friendship and walk in covenant relationship with believers from fellowships other than your own.

4. Join with those who call the church to unity.

Remember, harmony of relationship is a matter of the heart, not a structural problem. All relationship moves through a natural process and must be allowed to progress at its own pace:

Observation	Intimacy
Attraction	Fruitfulness
Courtship	Celebration
Covenant	

Lesson 9

Worship: The Place of Beginnings

This lesson covers Chapter 17, "Worship: The Place of Beginnings" (pages 161-168).

Notes to the Teacher

The objective of this lesson is to move from deep personal repentance over murmuring and self-pity into dynamic praise. Lead the group in a time of heartfelt confession followed by declarations of thanksgiving for all the privileges in our lives. This may be the time to bring instruments and to bless the Lord through anointed worship choruses.

I. Introduction

This lesson begins the fifth section, **Into Battle: Five Steps to Victory**. Worship is always the beginning point for a spiritual victory. We begin by looking away from our circumstances and up to God on high.

II. Look up! Then you will understand.

III. Thanksgiving vs. murmuring.

IV. The beauty of God's people.

V. A city of destiny.

VI. Here to stay unless God redirects me.

Vll. The glory revealed.

****

Everything born of God goes through a very natural process: worship, conception, gestation, travail and birth. It's in the place of thanksgiving and praise that God conceives within us His mind and heart for our city.

****

Notes to the Student

Questions for thoughtful reflection:
1. Do I look beyond the negative factors in my city? Do I see its redemptive potentials?

2. Am I here by accident or has God had His hand on my life all along? Did He locate me here?

3. Am I just surviving or am I walking into the inheritance that God has for me?

4. Am I living in faith or do I really believe that the negative things will never change?

5. Do I practise the discipline of thanksgiving as a way of life or is murmuring more natural to me?

6. Could I share a godly vision for my city's future if someone were to ask me what God is doing here?

Be involved by answering these questions:
1. How did King Jehoshaphat's army win the battle? (page 162)..
....

2. What are some of the negative effects of murmuring and complaining? (page 162)

....

....

3. Is praise an act of my will or is it something I do only when I feel like it?.......................................

....

4. What is our message to modern urban humanity? (page 165)...

....

5. What is meant by the term "sacrificial praise"? (page 162)...

....

APPLICATION TO DAILY LIVING

Thanksgiving is usually learned as the correct social response to the favours somebody does for us, but it is really much more than that. It is a discipline just like fasting or Bible meditation.

It is also a command, as we see in Ephesians 5:20, "giving thanks always for all things to God the Father in the name of our Lord Jesus Christ."

This week as you begin your daily appointments with God, get out a piece of paper and list all the blessings in your life. You will be surprised how long your list becomes as the Holy Spirit begins to lift the dark veil of self-pity from your mind.

Lesson 10

Beginning to See...
Waiting on God
for Insight

This lesson covers Chapter 18, "Waiting on the Lord for Insight" (pages 169-179).

Notes to the Teacher

The subject of divine guidance can become complex and controversial. Keep your discussion biblical and balanced.

In some ways divine guidance is a skill to be learned, but reassure your group that God's ability to communicate with His children is greater than our tendency to confuse and complicate our direction. If we are humble, He will get us where we are going.

I. Introduction

Spiritual battles are won by following revelation given by the Holy Spirit. If we listen to God with childlike dependency He will guide us into victory.

II. The God Who Speaks

III. A People Who Listen

IV. Knowing God's Voice

V. The Sin of Presumption

VI. Humility and Dependence

VII. Letting Jesus Lead

****

"My sheep hear My voice and they follow Me."
John 10:27

****

Notes to the Student

Questions for thoughtful reflection:
1. When I pray, do I sense God's direction or do I just bring Him my "shopping list?"

2. Do I spend enough time in God's presence getting to know Him?

3. How do I lead others in Christian work? Am I reporting God's vision or just my own good plans?

4. Do I seek God with intensity only when faced with crisis?

5. Do my family and friends see me as a person who is actively following the living Christ?

6. Have I always sensed that God has much more in mind for me than what I am now experiencing? "Lord, what are your best plans for my life?"

Be involved by answering these questions:
1. How do we distinguish between God's voice and that of our imagination or deceiving spirits? (page 178)

....

....

2. What was the lesson the Israelites learned at the city of Ai? (page 172)..
....

3. What is the sin of presumption? (page 172)
....
....

4. Why is interceding for others the best way to become familiar with God's voice? (page 173)....................
....

5. Why did the children of Israel have confidence in Joshua's leadership? (page 179).......................................
....

6. What is the basic strategy in spiritual warfare that undergirds all others? (page 179)................................
....

APPLICATION TO DAILY LIVING

Every believer experiences at times a dark night of the soul when God's presence seems distant and His voice is not heard. However, the greater part of our life is not lived that way.

The still small voice of the spirit of God within our spirit constantly reassures us when we are on the right path, and disturbs us when we head in the wrong direction.

There are only three possible influences on our spirit when we are quietly asking God for direction:

1. Our own imagination and desire.

2. Demonic interference.

3. The voice of God.

We can consciously yield our minds to the Holy Spirit's influence and take authority over the demonic kingdom when we pray; that leaves us secure in the knowledge that what we are receiving is from God.

Along with a thorough knowledge of the principles in God's Word, the greatest asset we can have is a familiarity with the voice of Jesus because we have spent so much time in His presence.

Practise the presence of God this week by including Him in even the small things of life. Converse with God in the way that you would fellowship with a loving earthly father.

Lesson 11

Identifying With the Sins of the City

This lesson covers Chapter 19, "Identifying With the Sins of the City" (pages 181-187).

Notes to the Teacher

When the group has discussed and grasped the concepts, move into a time of identificational repentance among the members of the class.

Don't force any issues, but do create the opportunity for confession and healing if members of the group represent the diversity of the city through gender, culture, race, denomination, vocation and so on.

I. Introduction

We are hearing that the problem is not primarily demons, but rather our need to qualify to inherit what God has worked out for us or to restore that which we have already inherited. We can bring cleansing and healing through repentance and obedience. "You shall raise up the foundations of many generations; And you shall be called the Repairer of the Breach, the Restorer of Streets to Dwell In" (Is. 58:12).

II. Lord, reveal Your glory!

III. How can I bless that which is unrighteous?

IV. Who will stand in the gap before Me for the city?

V. See the breaks in the wall: corporate and ancestral sin.

VI. Identificational Repentance

VII. Cleansing and Healing the Land

****

"Then those of Israelite lineage separated themselves from all foreigners; and they stood and confessed their sins and the iniquities of their fathers."

Nehemiah 9:2

****

Notes to the Student

Questions for thoughtful reflection:
1. Is there a subtle self-righteousness influencing the way I pray for others?

2. Have I seen the evil events and values of my city as a matter of shame before God?

3. Have I ever felt like apologising to the Lord because of the values of the culture around me?

4. Have I ever felt unresolved guilt because of what my ancestors did to God or to people in the past?

5. Have the people of my ethnic group, denomination, class or culture ever been guilty of oppressing another group in our society?

6. Is my prejudice a result of the unresolved guilt within my culture group?

Be involved by answering these questions:
1. Why did the people repent according to their category? (page 184)..
....

2. Why does an intercessor weep? (page 182)
....
....

3. How could a righteous man like Nehemiah say, "I and this people have sinned" (Neh. 1:6-7)?
....
....

4. Why is God looking for somebody to "stand in the gap?"...
....

5. Why is confession linked to healing and spiritual authority? (James 5:16, page 185)...
....

6. Can we see sin as God sees it, or do we need the assistance of the Holy Spirit in order to know the horror of sin, in order to truly humble ourselves?
....
....

APPLICATION TO DAILY LIVING

As we follow Jesus, we come out of deception into

truth. We begin to see ourselves as God sees us and to honestly confess sin before God and before others. As cleansing takes place, spiritual authority increases.

This week consciously ask God for a revelation of your heart as God sees it, just as David did (Ps. 139:23-24, page 185).

Ask God for conviction of sin to fall on the whole city. Invite the Holy Spirit to begin with us, the people of God.

There may be a location in your city where great injustice or cruelty has taken place. There may be an institution that has become oppressive and corrupt, or a once godly ministry may have lost its fire.

Ask God for a revelation of how He feels about these things, even if it means experiencing shame and remorse. Ask God what needs to be done in order to see His presence restored in the situation.

Satan's strongholds are really just places where restoration has not yet taken place.

Lesson 12

Overcoming Evil With Good

This lesson covers Chapter 20, "Overcoming Evil With Good" (pages 189-200).

Notes to the Teacher

Begin by reading the prison story on page 192. Discuss the three principles listed on that page. Then read and discuss the theological paragraphs at the bottom of page 197 and on page 198.

I. Introduction
When we have discerned the presence of a particular satanic strategy, we need to cultivate the opposite characteristic, not only through resisting temptation, but by demonstrating positive action and declaring Christ's victory on the cross.

II. Resisting Temptation

III. Taking Positive Action

IV. Creating With God

****

God allows Satan's attacks for three reasons: the Lord wants to build character in us, He wants to expose and defeat the enemy and He wants us to occupy territory for the kingdom which was once held by the powers of darkness.

****

Notes to the Student

Questions for thoughtful reflection:

1. Am I merely reacting to the enemy or am I destroying his works through Christ's power?

2. Have I ever declared with my mouth that Jesus is Lord of the city, that His authority is above all else?

3. Have I ever gained a spiritual victory in the midst of intense personal difficulties?

4. What temptations am I facing right now?

5. Do these temptations relate to the nature of a satanic stronghold in this town?

6. What action should I take in order to apply Christ's victory?

Be involved by answering these questions:

1. What did the author learn about God's authority in the prison? (page 195)...
....

2. Why is it important for a redeemed human to speak out the intention of God? (page 198).........................
....

3. Why can the accuser of our souls no longer condemn us?(page 198)..
....

4. What is the relationship between fasting and spiritual authority? (page 190)...
....

5. What is the principle of the "exchanged life"? (page 190)..
....

6. What purpose does temptation serve? (page 190)
....
....

7. Why is it crucial that the believer know and memorise Scripture? (page 198)...
....

APPLICATION TO DAILY LIVING

Overcoming evil with good is not a spiritual technique, but represents a means of applying the victory of Jesus. It's time to discern what is hindering us and to intensify prayer and action against it.

This week, stir up the gift of discerning of spirits. What is oppressing you and your neighbours? What positive actions could you take to resist the enemy in his strongholds?

Since Pentecost, we have become the dwelling place of God's Spirit. God wants us to think His thoughts, pray His prayers, feel His emotions, do His work and speak His words.

We speak in the name of Jesus, through the power of the Spirit, because of the shed blood of Jesus, with the sword of the Spirit which is the Word of God.

Lesson 13
Travailing Until Birth

This lesson covers Chapter 21, "Travailing Until Birth" (pages 201-217).

Notes to the Teacher

After discussing the concepts in this chapter, call upon each group member to express the commitment that God has called him to. This may require research on your part so that the group has current information about prayer movements, volunteer ministries and the scheduled prayer gatherings of the church.

I. Introduction

Having walked through this fascinating study of the theology and tactics of spiritual warfare, we now must focus on the commitment of prayer. Intercession must become a way of life. Remember, intercessory prayer involves worship, conception, gestation, travail, birth and celebration.

II. Seasons of Intensity

III. Praying Until. . .

IV. Healing the Broken Heart of God

V. A Heart of Flesh for a Heart of Stone

VI. Attentive Endurance

Vll. The Interceding Christ Takes Control

Vlll. The Fellowship of His Suffering

IX. Endurance: A Stubborn Faith

****

When you truly love somebody, you don't just mention that person before the Lord. You pray until that which is needed happens, until the answer comes, until breakthrough. Love settles for nothing less than victory. Love fills us with an earnest ambition for the desired result.

****

Notes to the Student

Questions for thoughtful reflection:

1. Have I nourished the godly hope that was put in my heart or have I aborted all God's words to me through impatience and unbelief?

2. What promises have I almost forgotten? Could it be that God in His faithfulness is still preparing me to inherit?

3. How much endurance have I demonstrated in praying for my loved ones?

4. Do I secretly resent God because some of my dreams have not come true?

5. Could it be that God has much more for me than the limited vision I now have for my life?

6. If not revival and harvest, then what?

7. Will continuing darkness and mediocrity cost me more than the disciplined path of obedience?

Be involved by answering these questions:

1. What two conditions affect the level of spiritual victory? (page 202)..
....

2. Why was Elisha so disappointed with the young king? (pages 202-203)...
....

3. What was Moses' first priority as a leader? (page 203)..
....

4. How has God made Himself vulnerable to us? (page 206)...
....

5. Why must we give the Holy Spirit access to our emotions? (page 207)...
....

6. How long did Abraham wait for the child of promise? (page 210)...
....

7. What lesson did the woman with the deliverance ministry learn? (page 211)..
....

APPLICATION TO DAILY LIVING

What are you going through right now? Maybe it's something easily resolved, but it could be one of those times when you need to endure in the circumstance until the character of Christ is formed in you, and you gain that needed place of spiritual authority.

Resurrection power comes only after the cross has done its work. Self-interest, self-promotion, self-preservation and self-consciousness have to die in order for us to experience the fullness of intimate friendship with a holy God, and to obtain overcoming authority in destroying the works of Satan.

No victory is instant. God is building within us an enduring faith that is not contingent upon the measure of our progress, the number of our resources or the strength of our allies. He often brings resurrection when all human strength is gone.

Know this. The pain of labour is soon forgotten in the joy of receiving that for which we have travailed. In a sense, our whole lives are a process of travail.

A few months ago my beloved father-in-law, Al, passed away. For all our sorrow, that memorial service still had the feeling of a graduation.

He had put off the veil of flesh just like a baby does when it is born; so shall I, and so shall you.

Let this also be a reminder that a life of prayer and obedience leaves a legacy of blessing for many generations. We ourselves are the fruit of the travail of saints long gone.

Let us pray for our children and the generations after them. Even if we do not see an answer with our eyes, He who is faithful is able to accomplish that which He said He would do.